BRITISH TOPOGRAPHICAL SERIES

THE FENLAND

THE FENLAND

Anthony Parker and
Denis Pye

David & Charles
Newton Abbot   London
North Pomfret (VT)   Vancouver

TO JOEY
IN MEMORIAM

ISBN 0 7153 7296 3

Library of Congress Catalog Card Number 76-29114

© A. K. Parker and D. Pye 1976

Set in 11 on 13pt Mallard
and printed in Great Britain
by A. Wheaton & Company, Exeter
for David & Charles (Publishers) Limited
Brunel House   Newton Abbot   Devon

Published in the United States of America
by David & Charles Inc
North Pomfret   Vermont 05053 USA

Published in Canada
by Douglas David & Charles Limited
1875 Welch Street   North Vancouver BC

Contents

1 Bardney 2 Tattershall 3 Mareham-le-Fen 4 Revesby 5 Old Bolingbroke 6 East Keal 7 Toynton All Saints 8 Stickford 9 Stickney 10 Sibsey 11 Friskney 12 Old Leake 13 Wrangle 14 Leverton 15 Freiston 16 Fishtoft 17 South Kyme 18 Heckington 19 Helpringham 20 Swaton 21 Horbling 22 Billingborough 23 Dowsby 24 Rippingale 25 Dunsby 26 Hacconby 27 Morton 28 Swineshead 29 Bicker 30 Donington 31 Quadring 32 Gosberton 33 Wyberton 34 Frampton 35 Kirton-in-Holland 36 Sutterton 37 Fosdyke 38 Surfleet 39 Pinchbeck 40 Weston 41 Moulton 42 Whaplode 43 Fleet 44 Gedney 45 Lutton 46 Long Sutton 47 Moulton Chapel 48 Thurlby 49 Baston 50 Langtoft 51 West Deeping 52 Market Deeping 53 Deeping St James 54 Maxey 55 Northborough 56 Glinton 57 Peakirk 58 Crowland 59 Thorney 60 Parson Drove 61 Tydd St Giles 62 Sutton Bridge 63 Terrington St Clement 64 Walpole St Andrew 65 Walpole St Peter 66 West Walton 67 Leverington 68 Walsoken 69 Terrington St John 70 Tilney All Saints 71 West Lynn 72 Castle Rising 73 North Runcton 74 Wiggenhall St Mary the Virgin 75 Wiggenhall St Germans 76 Wiggenhall St Mary Magdalen 77 Wormegay 78 Runcton Holme 79 Stow Bardolph 80 Wimbotsham 81 Guyhirne 82 Elm 83 Emneth 84 Outwell 85 Upwell 86 Nordelph 87 Denver 88 West Dereham 89 Oxborough 90 Hilgay 91 Southery 92 Northwold 93 Methwold 94 Feltwell 95 Hockwold-cum-Wilton 96 Lakenheath 97 Longthorpe 98 Fletton 99 Yaxley 100 Holme 101 Conington 102 Wood Walton 103 Bury 104 Warboys 105 Somersham 106 Bluntisham 107 Earith 108 Fenstanton 109 Fen Drayton 110 Swavesey 111 Over 112 Willingham 113 Rampton 114 Cottenham 115 Impington 116 Landbeach 117 Fen Ditton 118 Horningsea 119 Waterbeach 120 Lode 121 Bottisham 122 Swaffham Prior 123 Reach 124 Burwell 125 Fordham 126 Chippenham 127 Isleham 128 Soham 129 Wicken 130 Stuntney 131 Prickwillow 132 Downham-in-the-Isle 133 Coveney 134 Witchford 135 Little Thetford 136 Stretham 137 Wilburton 138 Haddenham 139 Sutton-in-the-Isle 140 Witcham 141 Wentworth 142 Manea 143 Doddington 144 Wimblington 145 Benwick 146 Cowbit 147 Swaffham Bulbeck 148 Cherry Hinton 149 Mepal

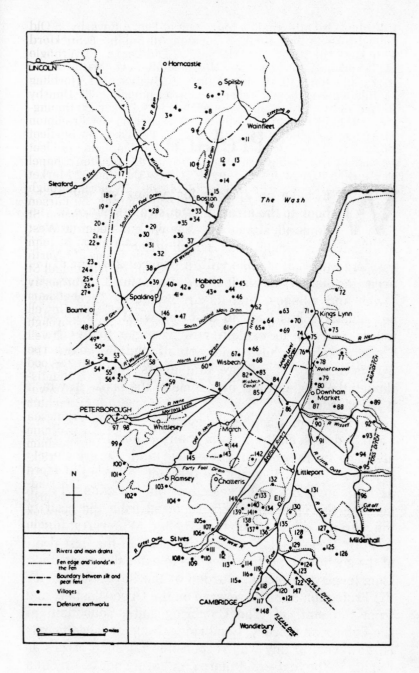

Map of the the Fenland today

Preface

WE make no apology for adding yet one more book to the already extensive literature on the Fenland, simply because we have been unable to discover a single book which attempts to provide resident and visitor alike with a *general* account of the area: its history, its agriculture, its natural history, its towns and villages, and its architecture. Throughout, our objective has been to describe what is to be seen today, and try to explain how it came to be there. Consequently we have said virtually nothing about the extensive store of folklore that exists about the Fens, though the Bibliography lists some of the books in which it is recorded.

Inevitably, in compiling a synthesis of this kind, we have had to seek the help of many experts. They have given us freely of their knowledge and we are deeply grateful to them. It would be difficult to list all of them and it is invidious to be selective, but we cannot fail to mention the particular help received from the staff of the various divisions of the Anglian Water Authority, from Dr Hope-Taylor (whose criticisms of the first draft of the section on archaeology led to extensive rewriting), from Jeremy Sorenson, warden of the Royal Society for the Protection of Birds reserve on the Ouse Washes, and from the staff of 'The Cambridgeshire Collection' at the Reference Library, Cambridge. None of these people is, however, in any way responsible for such errors as remain in the text—and there can hardly not be any in a work that attempts to paint so broad a canvas.

Finally, we express our gratitude to Janet Pye who typed almost the entire book, most of it from extremely messy manuscript, to David Beard, who took photographs especially for us, and to our families for the forbearance they have shown during a very long gestation period.

Cambridge and Coveney
August 1975

Anthony Parker
Denis Pye

1 Introduction

THE Great Level of the Fens occupies an area of about 1,300 square miles in eastern England. It extends from Cambridge in the south to Lincoln in the north, and from the Cambridgeshire-Suffolk boundary in the east to within a few miles of Stamford in the west.

To the west and north, it is bounded by the limestone ridge that runs from the west Dorset coast across England to the Humber estuary and of which the Lincoln Cliff is part. To the east and south lies the chalk ridge that runs from east Dorset to the Norfolk coast, forming on the way the Downs of Berkshire and Wiltshire and the Chiltern Hills. Between the two ridges in the south is a narrow belt of clay which, in the Fenland itself, is hidden beneath the surface soils.

The Wash intrudes between the limestone and the chalk in the north. In this bay of shifting sands are the outfalls of the Fenland rivers, the Witham, the Welland, the Nene and the Great Ouse and their tributaries, rivers which between them drain a large part of midland England and have a catchment area about four times the area of the Fenland itself.

The surface soils are either peat or silt. In the southern fens, that is those lying in the enlarged county of Cambridgeshire, and also along the western edge of the Lincolnshire fens, the top soil is peat. Almost everywhere else it is silt, silt deposited by the ancient rivers along the Lincolnshire coast and in that part of Norfolk which lies between the estuaries of the Nene and the Ouse.

'Islands' and peninsulas of greensand or boulder clay obtrude through the surface soils in many places. Several of the Fenland towns and villages are built on such islands, their names often having the Old English ending –ey or –ea, meaning an island. Among them are Ramsey, Thorney, Coveney, Stickney, Sibsey, Manea, Whittlesey, Swavesey and Stuntney. The largest of these 'islands' is 10 miles across and rises to a height of 120ft above the level of the surrounding peat. On it stands the town of Ely and several villages and until it was drained it also included an isolated fen (Grunty Fen) within its boundaries.

Apart from these 'islands', the Fens are absolutely flat; flat but never featureless. There are always some trees to be seen: poplars standing like sentinels in rows, willows along a river bank, or clumps of older deciduous trees around an isolated farmstead, a church or an entire village, screening it from the winds in winter and providing shade in the summer. Grassy banks cut straight across the landscape, lining the sides of the rivers or the main drains, the level of which is often above that of the surrounding fields. A patchwork of smaller dykes divides the landscape into fields.

The flatness of the Fens stimulates the observer in a way that is hard to explain. The late Dr Vaughan Cornish, in his book *The Beauties of Scenery*, attributes this to the fact that, since the elevation of objects in the landscape is so slight, the observer unconsciously looks upwards, with the result that the sky occupies more of the view than it normally does, so increasing his sense of spaciousness.

Dr Cornish also tells the story of a Highland game-keeper travelling by train near Ely on his first visit to southern England. He was plainly thrilled by the sense of space in the same way that most of us are thrilled by the sense of height when we first see mountains, and was led to exclaim 'whichever way I look, there is nothing to interfere with the view!'

INTRODUCTION

The fen is always alive: lapwings wheel, reeds sway in the breeze and tractors thread their way repeatedly across the horizon, breaking the silence with their unnatural clatter. The very spaciousness of the fens encourages wildlife and birds, plants and insects have not been slow to take advantage of it.

The roads follow the dykes and run straight or perhaps zig-zag across the countryside, with sudden sharp bends which are a hazard to the stranger driving across the fen at night or in the fog. A few roads follow a more windy course on top of an old fen bank or the silted-up course of an old river.

The railways came later, driving straight across the fen and bridging the rivers and dykes wherever they met them. Where road and rail meet there is usually a level crossing, served in the past by a family living in a characteristic single-storey crossing keeper's house, but now more likely to have a set of automatic gates.

In these days of motor boats, pleasure traffic on the rivers is hidden by the banks on either side but, with luck, one may see the apparently detached mast and sails of one of the few remaining cruising yachts on the Fenland rivers gliding across the landscape.

Pumping stations are a prominent feature, since unlike farms and villages, they are rarely screened by belts of trees. The characteristic tripartite shape of the steam pumping station or that of its smaller, but more efficient, diesel or electric successor can often be seen near the banks of the rivers and main drains, particularly in the southern fens.

In the peat areas, farms and cottages often cling to the gravel or clay banks of the rivers, where they are able to find a firmer foundation than on the soft decaying peat. The roads that serve them follow the riverbanks closely, so that the weight of the traffic may help to consolidate the banks and prevent the river water seeping through into the low-lying fields.

The pumping stations, dykes and banks are the visible

evidence that the Fenland landscape, as it is today, is completely man-made. Without the continual building and maintenance of riverbanks, the clearing of drains and the pumping of water from the drains into the rivers, the Fenland would be utterly different from the country we know today. It would become once more, as it was in early medieval times, a great marsh, teeming with wildlife no doubt, but contributing virtually nothing to the feeding of the 50 million people who now live in Britain.

The story of the struggle to convert the marshy ague-ridden wastes into highly productive farmland and orchards is one of the most fascinating in the history of Britain. It is the visible evidence of this story that gives to the Fenland its unique character. Its attraction may be less obvious to the casual visitor than are the lakes and mountains of Cumbria or the rocky coastline of Cornwall, but to those who have time to stand and stare and are willing to search for its secrets, the Fenland has as much to offer as any other part of Britain.

Everywhere in this man-made landscape, history is displayed. Nor does the matter stop there, for effective land drainage is an activity which demands co-operation between even the most independent of men. Thus the co-operation of neighbours facing the common risk of flooding, led eventually to the formulation of an overall plan and to the institution of an authority to carry it out. So the history of fen drainage is also a history of the development of human institutions, leading ultimately to the formation of a single water authority for the whole of eastern England, the logical finale of a development that began with the appointment of the first Commission of Sewers in 1258.

Agriculture is still the primary industry in the Fens, and many of the other industries—food processing, canning and freezing, jam making and the manufacture and distribution of fertilisers, feeding stuffs and machinery—depend heavily on it. It is far from being a static industry. Fenland agriculture has steadily adapted itself to its environment and to the requirements of an increasingly sophisticated market. No doubt in future it will continue to introduce new crops, to try out new varieties of present ones and to take full advantage of innovations in machinery and other equipment.

2   The Fenland in Prehistoric and Roman Times

The Landscape

THE history of the Fenland is quite unlike that of any other part of Britain. It is a history of a changing landscape in a situation where comparatively small fluctuations in sea-level have been the cause of major changes in the wetness of the land and consequently in its habitability, and where battles and politics take second place to the works of nature and the activity of the settlers and the engineers.

The story has been pieced together by scientists, historians and archaeologists. Much can be learnt from aerial photography, in which the pattern of earlier layouts is highlighted by the relief, by soil marks and by the differential growth of crops. On the ground, the application of the techniques of pollen analysis and radiocarbon dating to the various layers of soil, provides information about the climate and vegetation at different periods of time. The remains of animals and the artifacts (weapons, tools, pots, coins etc) unearthed by archaeologists enable them to build up a picture of human activity during each period.

The story begins at the time of the last ice age in Britain, about 10,000 years ago, when the retreating ice left a plain in eastern England in the area between the two great geological belts which cross England from the Dorset coast to the Humber estuary. These belts, the oolitic limestone of the Cotswold country and the chalk of the Downs and the Chilterns, are adjacent in the south of England and come together again in Lincoln-shire. At that time the Wash did not exist and the chalk escarpment was continuous, being broken only by the valleys through which the predecessors of the Fenland rivers emptied themselves into the sea, which was at that time far away to the north.

The Fenland plain was an area of clay and gravel, with wide river valleys and much woodland, principally pine and birch. As the climate grew warmer and wetter, other trees became established, especially oak, lime, alder and, later, beech; the valleys became waterlogged, leading to the formation of the first layers of peat.

Fen carr, a dense thicket composed chiefly of buck-thorn and alder buckthorn, formed on top of the peat. As it decayed, seeds from the surrounding woodlands established themselves in the bare patches and the fen became an extension of the woodland. However, as the peat dried out and shrank, the roots of the trees became waterlogged, in some places with salt water, and they died. This is the origin of the so-called bog oaks found all over the peat fens: trees (not necessarily oaks) buried under the peat which are now coming to the surface again as the well-drained peat decays.

A drier period followed but sometime between 1300 and 300 BC there was an inundation by the sea. This could perhaps have been caused by the wearing away of the chalk barrier across what is now the Wash, combined with a general rise in sea level in relation to that of the land. Silts and clays were deposited in what had become a great inland sea, with the higher ground forming islands.

On the seaward side there was a large area of mud flats forming an estuary which penetrated inland as far as Littleport. The rivers were strongly tidal and silts were carried up the natural watercourses by the flood tide to form ridges (levées) on either side of the channel; due to the lack of fall, the ebbtide was comparatively weak and the silt was not therefore carried away as fast as it was deposited. In this way the roddons were formed; today they may stand at a level above that of the shrunken peat, and often provide firm foundations for buildings or even whole villages. Their existence makes it comparatively easy to trace the courses of the rivers which flowed through Fenland during the Iron Age (which began about 500 BC) and the subsequent period of the Roman occupation. One of the best known roddons is the old course of the Ouse east of Ely and Prickwillow. Where this is crossed by the Prickwillow to Shippea Hill road (TL 612849), a large dyke cuts through the roddon, so that a complete profile of it may be seen in the dyke side.

At this time also, meres were formed in areas in which there was sufficient movement of water to prevent conditions becoming stagnant and the growth of vegetation. The formation of *Chara* marl, a white chalky material derived from freshwater algae, in the meres gave rise to the name White Fens. The larger ones, some of which survived until the nineteenth century, are shown on the map of the Fenland in Roman times (Fig 1 p 25).

Levées of *Chara* marl formed by streams entering the fens from the chalk hills to the east are known as slades although in other respects they are similar to roddons. One such slade is the line of the former Roman canal from Reach to Upware.

The period of the Roman occupation (AD 43-410) was one of comparatively intensive settlement and major change in Fenland. There is evidence of large-scale and effective planning of a kind not seen again until the seventeenth century: roads and canals were built, rivers diverted and many settlements established, particularly on the silt land of south Lincolnshire.

The arrival of the Romans seems to have coincided with the start of a drier climatic phase and the end of the period of deposition of the estuarine clays on top of the peat that had been proceeding throughout the Iron Age and perhaps earlier. Settlement in the Fenland began about AD 70-80 and was at its peak during the first half of the second century. Later there seems to have been an economic depression, probably arising from the unsettled state of the Roman Empire at that time, accompanied by some freshwater flooding. A recovery followed towards the end of the third century, and prosperity was maintained until the end of the Roman era.

This pattern argues for the existence of a large-scale drainage system which fell into decay at times of economic depression and weak government. Some of the canals which are either definitely or probably Roman seem to have been built solely for transport purposes, while others, by shortening the courses of the winding rivers, increased their rate of flow and so carried the water away to the sea more effectively. They represent the beginnings of the river system we know today, in which, for the larger part of their courses, the Fenland rivers follow straight artificial channels rather than winding natural ones.

In Roman times, the four main river systems in the southern Fenland were the Nene, which flowed into the Wash north of Wisbech; the Ouse, which wound its way north from Earith as the West Water to join the Old Nene, entering the Wash at Wisbech; the Cam, which also flowed to Wisbech, though taking a less direct route in the vicinity of Ely than it does today; and finally the Nar and a short unnamed river, which found their exit to the sea at King's Lynn, having no connection at that time with the other Fenland rivers.

We do not know when the river system took its present shape, but it is not impossible that the Romans built the Littleport–Brandon Creek Cut and the Ten Mile Bank River and so made the first move in diverting part of the water which had hitherto flowed into the sea at Wisbech to the King's Lynn estuary.

The Romans also began the reclamation of the silt-lands of south Lincolnshire. There, the heavily populated settlements were linked by networks of fields which moved out towards the sea as new land was formed and secured by banks, replacing the peaty land further behind which was subject to freshwater flooding from the Fenland itself.

Prehistoric People

Even before the ice finally departed, man had left his traces in the Fenland. In this, the Palaeolithic period, man was a hunter who moved about from place to place, so that evidence of settlement is scanty. The concentration of flint axes and other artefacts is greatest in the river valleys, particularly those of the Little Ouse and Lark, and near Mildenhall a site has been excavated which appears to have been a primitive axe factory from which nearly 8,000 flint specimens were recovered.

The Mesolithic (Middle Stone Age) period which followed the Ice Age is also represented on the eastern fen edge and at other sites on sandy hillocks in the Ely fens. An important site has been uncovered at Peacock's Farm, Shippea Hill, where the microliths (small stone points and sharp edges for mounting on tools and weapons) show similarities to continental examples, but could equally well be the result of independent development. This site is now 17ft below sea level, an indication of the amount by which the land has sunk relative to the sea since about 5000 BC.

Before 3000 BC, the first farmers arrived in the Fenland. These Neolithic peoples came from southern England, travelling up both sides of the Fens and settling in the river valleys and along the fen edge, where they found light and well-drained soils which were relatively easy to cultivate with primitive tools. They belonged to the Windmill Hill culture, which takes its name from the causewayed camp in Wiltshire where it was first identified.

Most of the sites on which they settled have since been intensively farmed or quarried for gravel, so few examples remain of their insubstantial dwellings, or of the wedge-shaped unchambered long barrows in which they buried their dead. Recently, however, some major sacred monuments have been excavated by the Welland Valley Research Committee, the largest being at Maxey, where a number of small round sanctuaries are grouped round an avenue over a mile long. In one of the sanctuaries, an unexpected find was three antlers bearing elaborately engraved and painted designs, probably being intended for use in religious ceremonies held on the site.

On the other side of the Fens, an early Neolithic site at Hurst Fen, near Mildenhall, has proved to be a workshop for the production of flint tools. It also yielded evidence of corn-growing and of trade, since polished stone axes from the Lake District were found there.

A later Neolithic culture seems to have spread into the Fenland from the east. It takes its name from ceramic ware discovered on a low gravel ridge at Fengate on the east side of Peterborough. Such Peterborough ware is heavy and coarse, and is usually covered with impressed decoration; it is to be found all over England, in Wales and in southern Scotland.

Flint axes from the mines at Grimes Graves, Norfolk (TL 816898) are, not surprisingly, well represented among those found in the southern Fenland. It is now thought that the mines were intensively worked about 2000 BC by people of the Windmill Hill culture, which continued alongside later Neolithic cultures such as that of Peterborough.

About 2000 BC eastern and southern England were invaded by the Beaker people, so-called on account of their distinctive bell-shaped drinking vessels, often decorated with horizontal bands bearing incised geometric patterns. Among the many beakers in the Cambridge Museum of Archaeology and Ethnology are two fine decorated beakers with handles, shaped like modern beer mugs, from Bottisham and Fordham. The Beaker people were probably the first of the many groups of invaders who made use of the Fenland rivers to reach drier settlement sites in the interior. It was the Beaker people who first introduced the use of metal into England and they are therefore regarded as an intermediate culture between the Neolithic Age and the Bronze Age proper.

The Beaker people buried their dead in cemeteries (there was one at Ely) or sometimes beneath round barrows, a custom which continued during the Bronze Age. Most surviving Bronze Age barrows are on the higher ground around the edge of the fens, well away from the destructive influence of the plough or the gravel scoop. One exception is the very large barrow that has recently been excavated at Tallington in the Welland valley. It seems to have been the site of a series of burials, the mound being enlarged after each one until its diameter reached 170ft (52m); the contents of this and a neighbouring barrow indicate that they were built about 1700 BC.

A few Middle Bronze Age barrows have also been found in the fens themselves, eg at Mepal, providing further evidence that the land must then have been relatively higher and drier. Towards the end of the Bronze Age, however, trackways were constructed across the low-lying ground between Stuntney and Ely and between Little Thetford and Barway, so the situation had evidently deteriorated by that time.

The most extensive Bronze Age settlement yet known in the Fens is being excavated at Fengate by a team of archaeologists from the Royal Ontario Museum in Canada. An elaborate system of fields, droves and ditches has been revealed, indicating that agriculture contributed substantially to an economy based on the products of the fen (fish, eels, wildfowl and peat) and the summer grazing it provided.

Some superb examples of Bronze Age metalwork have been discovered in the Fens and the total number of finds of all kinds is very great indeed. Most of these finds have been attributed to the Late Bronze Age, including several bronzesmiths' hoards. One of these hoards of material for melting down and recasting was found in a pottery-lined pit at Isleham and contained no fewer than 6,500 pieces of metal, weighing over 200lb.

Bronze casting techniques were basically similar to those employed in modern foundries, though there was relatively poor control over the composition of the alloy. The technique of permanent mould casting (or gravity die casting as it is sometimes called) using metal moulds, which is applied to aluminium alloys today, was used for casting axes and other items required in quantity.

Hoards of finished objects probably belonged to merchants or were in private possession; finds at Wilburton and Downham Market come into this category and the contents of a number of these hoards are displayed in the Cambridge Museum. Other finds comprised only one or two objects; these may perhaps have been votive offerings, deposited in rivers and swamps to propitiate the gods, or may simply have been lost in battle, in crossing rivers and so on.

The first iron-using peoples came to eastern England from the Low Countries about 500 BC, their cultural background being that associated with the site at Hallstatt in Austria. They settled on the edge of the fens and on the fen islands, as they found the rest of the area too wet at this period. They seem to have integrated themselves fairly easily with the Late Bronze Age peoples and occupied some of the same sites, for example, that at Fengate. Their swords, whether of bronze or iron, were narrow rather than leaf-shaped and their pottery bore bold geometric patterns.

A second group of invaders, which brought a much more highly developed Iron Age culture to Britain about 250 BC, came from the Marne region of France. Their culture, the La Tène, represented a fusion between the earlier Hallstatt culture and those of Greece and Rome, peoples with whom the Hallstatt Celts fought and traded.

The La Tène aristocracy was powerful and absolute, and given to lavish personal display. Their weapons and other possessions were of very high quality. The river Witham has yielded a magnificent bronze shield, an iron sword with curvilinear bronze scabbard ornament (both in the British Museum) and a bronze trumpet, while a burial of a chieftain at Cambridge was accompanied by elaborate personal ornaments: a bangle, brooch and a harness mounting, all of which are now in the Cambridge Museum. A similar burial near Mildenhall contained an iron sword, an axe, a gold torque and the skeletons of two chariot ponies. Once again, little is known of the settlements of the La Tène peoples, but a brushwood platform of piles at Fletton may have formed part of a lake village, similar to the well-known ones at Glastonbury and Meare in Somerset.

In the second century BC, a number of Belgic tribes crossed the Channel and settled in south-east England, from which area the Catuvellauni, in particular, spread northwards as far as the southern Fens. Others may have entered Lincolnshire by way of the Humber estuary and penetrated southwards; certainly Belgic coinage and wheel-turned pottery have been found at sites near the Lincolnshire fen edge and there was a mint at Old Sleaford. Another Belgic importation was a heavy plough with a wheel and coulter, capable of tackling heavy clay soils.

The grave of a Belgic chieftain at Snailwell sheds light on the customs of these people. The chieftain had been cremated and his ashes buried with his weapons and with food and drink to provide for his material needs in the next world. The pottery, which included amphorae for wine, was mostly from Gaul, of the first century AD. The contents of this grave are in the Cambridge Museum.

The high ground near the Fens is crowded with very few of those hill-top forts which are so characteristic of the Iron Age in Wessex and south-east England. Sites exist at Careby [TF 040156] and Honington [SK 954423] in Lincolnshire, Narborough [TF 752131] in Norfolk, and Wandlebury [TL 493534] in Cambridgeshire, though none is very near the fen edge. Excavations at Wandlebury have shown that it was originally constructed in the third century BC, possibly at the time of the La Tène invasions, and was later rebuilt and strengthened, perhaps as a defence against the Belgae. The second, inner, rampart and ditch which were constructed then, have since been destroyed, but the outer ditch remains today. Another camp, the so-called War Ditches, on an adjacent hill, was never completed but was destroyed by attackers who buried the bodies of the defenders in the ditch.

The Romans

The system of direct metalled (but not necessarily paved) roads which made it possible for the Romans to control their vast empire was extended into southern Britain in the years following the Roman conquest in AD 43.

The fact that some of the roads shown in Fig 1 ran across low-lying parts of the Fens is clear evidence that the Fens were comparatively dry for at least part of the Roman period. It seems likely that Akeman Street, the Cambridge–Ely–Denver road, was regarded as an easy route from the south into north-east Norfolk, thus making it unnecessary to convert the prehistoric Icknield Way, north of Worstead Lodge, into a metalled road.

THE FENLAND IN PREHISTORIC AND ROMAN TIMES

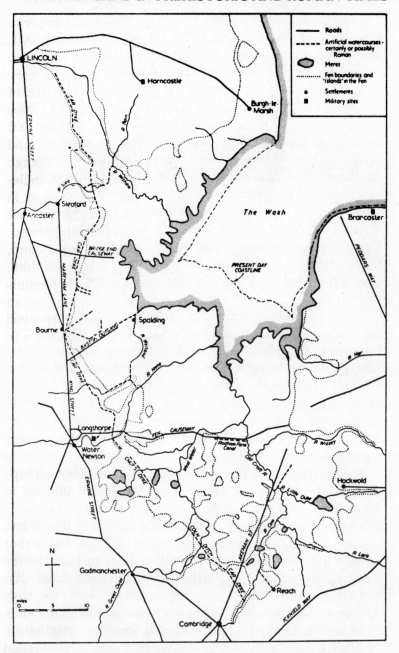

Fig 1   The Fenland in Roman times

The roads running eastwards from the limestone belt towards the Lincolnshire coast do not appear to lead anywhere today. The most northerly of these, which ran in an arc from Lincoln, across the wolds, to beyond Burgh-le-Marsh may very well have led to a Saxon Shore fort which has now disappeared beneath the sea; local references to Chesterland or Casterland, prior to 1422, strongly suggest a Roman settlement there. Some writers have suggested that there was a ferry across the Wash from this site to the end of the Peddars Way, the Roman Road running south to Colchester.

Of the two roads which crossed rather than skirted the Lincolnshire fens, the Baston Outgang probably led to the numerous Roman sites near Spalding, while the destination of the Bridge End Causeway can only be guessed at: was it a port, a fort or a centre of the salt industry?

There are very few military settlements in the Fenland area about which we can be certain, if we consider the important provincial capital and legionary fortress at Lincoln to be outside the area. These are the first-century campaign fortress at Longthorpe recently discovered by aerial photography, a fort on the outskirts of the pottery town of Durobrivae (Water Newton), a few miles further up the Nene valley, and another at Cambridge.

The settlement of the fens seems to have been highly organised and several writers have suggested that they formed an imperial estate, under the direct control of the emperor. The tasks of providing effective drainage and of bringing into production land which had not been settled for over 500 years were too large to have been undertaken piecemeal. Furthermore, the most intensive period of settlement coincided with a visit by the Emperor Hadrian, who is known to have taken comparable action to deal with neglected imperial estates in North Africa.

Villas of the kind which would form the centre of

large farming estates were concentrated around the fen edges; very few sites have been found in the fens themselves. The rest of the estates comprised small scattered farms consisting of enclosures containing rectangular thatched huts of timber, wattle and daub, connected by droveways to fields and pastures. Besides the farmhouse, such a settlement usually included a granary, racks for drying corn, and hollows for threshing, milling and cooking. At Sleaford, corn-drying kilns have been discovered. Cereals, cattle and pigs were the main products.

In the later Roman period, the settlements seem to have been larger, probably as a result of the natural growth of the family unit in a period of peace and prosperity. Sometimes, as in the large settlement excavated at Hockwold, a villa was associated with a particular village in the way that a manor house later formed part of a medieval village. There were also a number of pottery kilns in the Fenland, making wares for the local population.

The Nene valley seems to have been an important industrial centre in Roman times. A major pottery industry was established at Water Newton about AD 150, and was in large-scale production by AD 200. It was especially noted for its colour coated ware—fine pottery with a dark lustrous coat—which was exported by waterway and road to all parts of Britain. Examples may be seen in the British Museum, and in museums at Cambridge and Peterborough. Iron mining and smelting were carried on at Wansford, further up the valley, and the stone quarries at Barnack were also worked then.

The evaporation of sea water to provide salt was a flourishing industry on the north Lincolnshire coast during the Iron Age and the Romans seem to have extended it to sites in the Fenland. Here the salterns are mostly sited near the tidal limit of seawater creeks, close to the necessary supplies of peat fuel. Such sites may today be as far inland as Denver and Runcton Holme.

Apart from the roads and the canals, the Roman occupation left few marks on the Fenland. There is nothing to be seen of any of the excavated buildings, though their contents are preserved in museums and fragments of a mosaic pavement from the villa at Landwade may be seen at Cambridge. The quality of the finds is ample evidence that a minority of the inhabitants of Roman Britain were wealthy enough to indulge a taste for beautiful objects.

Among the finest individual finds are the Christian pewter *tazza* from Sutton (Cambridge), the bronze skillet from Prickwillow with its stamped ornamental handle bearing the maker's name *Bodnogenus*, the bronze statuette of Mars from Earith, the bronze helmet from Witcham, and the bronze crown and diadems from Hockwold (all in the British Museum).

The most remarkable finds of all are the hoards, mostly dating from the end of the Roman occupation, probably buried by their owners in those troubled times, or perhaps during the disaster of AD 367, and never recovered. They include the amazing Mildenhall treasure housed in the British Museum, comprising 34 pieces of very high quality silver tableware, the largest being a dish nearly two feet in diameter and weighing over 18lb. The finer pieces were certainly imported, but some of the others could have been made in Britain.

Among other hoards dating from the end of the fourth century AD are 14 bronze vessels found at Burwell, 865 coins found at Tiled House Farm, Stretham, and 30 gold coins from Water Newton. Several hoards of pewter tableware—dishes, cups, plates and bowls—have also been discovered.

The English Settlement and the Dark Ages

Although we may never know exactly what happened in Britain after the Roman troops finally withdrew in

AD 407 and the imperial administrators left three years later, recent archaeological research taken together with the few written records does yield a plausible picture of the situation, at least as far as eastern England is concerned.

The close association of pagan Germanic cemeteries with fortified Roman towns in Lincolnshire, Cambridgeshire and Norfolk and the presence in them of cremation urns similar to continental examples of the mid-fourth century AD, as well as of later periods, suggest that the first Germanic settlers came to Britain many years before the departure of the Romans. Possibly they were mercenaries invited by Count Theodosius when he was given the task of reorganising the defences following the concerted attack on Roman Britain in AD 367 by the Saxons, Picts and Scots.

Twenty years of prosperity followed the Roman withdrawal and then there were attacks by the Irish and the Picts, which were only defeated with the help of further groups of invited Germanic soldiers. Gildas and other writers tell us that, in AD 442 or thereabouts, the Germanic settlers revolted against their paymasters and obtained control of Norfolk and, ultimately, other parts of eastern Britain.

Gildas also tells us that, following the battle of Mons Badonicus about the year AD 500, Romano-British rule was restored in some areas and there was then a period of peace. The evidence of the cremation urns supports this, as some cemeteries show a break in the typology of the urns compared with contemporary continental examples. Since this break does not occur in the Fenland, we must conclude that the Germanic settlers did not withdraw from there. On the other hand, neither was the earliest civilisation completely wiped out, even by the end of the Dark Ages, as St Guthlac mentions the existence of Celtic-speaking Britons in the Fens as late as AD 700.

Further waves of Germanic settlers arrived during the

sixth century AD and the historic kingdoms emerged then: the East Angles in Suffolk and Norfolk, and the Middle Angles and the other kingdoms which later coalesced to form the kingdom of Mercia to the west and north of the Fens.

Although there are several of these Germanic cemeteries of the pagan period around the Fens and a few on fen islands, there are none in the fens themselves. Indeed, the rich Fenland farms seem to have been abandoned early in the fifth century. The likely explanation is that the rise in the sea level led to flooding which it was then beyond the power of the administration to counter. It is difficult to believe that, with additional settlers to accommodate, any good agricultural land would have been left unoccupied unless conditions prevented its use.

Not all Germanic burials during the period AD 350-650 were cremations and some cemeteries contained both cremations and inhumations. In the latter, men are found buried with their weapons and food, and women in woollen clothes bearing ornaments. Sleaford was the site of one of the largest mixed cemeteries in Britain, with over 600 burials.

Evidence from settlements is very slender. A late Dark Age settlement at Maxey in the Welland valley has been excavated; it comprised a number of rectangular timber buildings at ground level, not sunk in the fashion of similar buildings elsewhere. Pottery was once again hand made rather than turned on a wheel, the shapes being comparatively crude and the decoration coarse. Metalwork preserved in museums comes mostly from cemeteries and includes bronze hanging bowls and various kinds of brooches and similar ornaments.

With the fens once again under water, the Roman roads across them became unusable and the Icknield Way returned to its previous importance as the route to and from East Anglia. In Cambridgeshire the chalk ridge along which the Icknield Way ran was bounded on the west by undrained fen and on the east by impenetrable forest. Across this neck of land are two gigantic earthworks, each comprising a ditch and a bank. The most northerly, the Devil's Dyke, is 7½ miles long and measures about 60ft from the bottom of the ditch to the top of the bank (as shown in Pl 2, p 34). The main part of the Fleam Dyke is over 3 miles long and of similar proportions to the Devil's Dyke. Its western end rests on Fulbourn Fen and there was a further section (since destroyed) between that and the river Cam at Fen Ditton. Three other defensive earthworks across the Icknield Way to the south-west of the Fleam Dyke are unrelated to the Fens and are poorly preserved.

We do not know for certain when or by whom these earthworks were constructed. The excavation of the Devil's Dyke by Dr Hope-Taylor in 1973 has showed that it could not have been constructed before AD 360 since a coin minted then was found buried in it. He also found evidence of the use of sophisticated engineering techniques in its construction. The Romans were undoubtedly capable of such building, but it is more likely that both dykes were built by the East Angles during the frontier wars with the Middle Angles and the Mercians in the late sixth and seventh centuries AD. It was at the end of this restless period that the monks of Ely came to Cambridge by boat in search of a stone coffin in which to place the body of their foundress, St Etheldreda, and found the city deserted and in ruins.

There are two lesser known linear earthworks in west Norfolk: the Launditch (also confusingly called the Devil's Dyke) and the Foss Ditch. Both run across the necks of peninsulas obtruding into the fens, the first from Narborough to Beachamwell and the second from Northwold to Weeting. Their objective seems to have been to defend as large an area of ground as possible with the minimum of labour. Their date is uncertain, though they cannot be earlier than AD 390.

3 Draining the Fens

AT some time after the departure of the Romans, either the land subsided or the sea rose once more and there was extensive flooding. In Spalding, for example, Romano-British debris has been found buried under several feet of estuarine silt and it is known that there was a comparable land subsidence in London during this period.

Apart from the islands, the southern Fens remained as fenland for the next thousand years until the large scale drainage schemes were carried out in the seventeenth century. Bede, writing in the year 731, gives us a picture of the Isle of Ely at that time as being 'surrounded on all sides by sea and fens' and resembling 'an island surrounded by water and marshes', deriving 'its name from the vast quantity of eels that are caught in the marshes'. The monk Felix in his *Life of St Guthlac* gives a similar but more detailed picture of 'a most dismal fen of immense size, which begins at the banks of the river Granta not far from the camp which is called Cambridge, and stretches from the south as far north as the sea. It is a very long tract, now consisting of marshes, now of bogs, sometimes of black waters overhung by fog, sometimes studded with wooded islands and traversed by the windings of tortuous streams'. The population was low and the whole region formed a no-man's-land between the kingdoms of Mercia and East Anglia.

Some idea of what the medieval peat fens were like

Plate 1 Lincolnshire: Heckington Church from the south-west. Decorated work at its best, superbly built in Ancaster stone (*A. F. Kersting*)

Plate 2 (above) Archaeologists at work on the Devil's Dyke in 1973, in advance of the building of the Newmarket bypass. The vast size of this earthwork, which stretches for 7½ miles from fen to forest, is brought out in the photograph (*Anglia Television*)

Plate 3 (below) Soham Lode: excavators at work widening the lode and driving in piles to prevent erosion of the banks. The work of maintaining the channels and floodbanks in the Fens is never-ending (*K. A. Hitch*)

can be gained from a visit to Wicken Sedge Fen today. Here the National Trust maintains, in something approaching its historic condition, the only part of the Fens which has never been drained, since it was kept as the common land of the people of Wicken from which they obtained sedge and reeds for thatching and turf for fuel. Today, however, it stands several feet above the level of the adjacent peat lands since these have been drained and cultivated, and in parts the peat is as much as 18ft thick. Also, the regular cutting of the sedge and the keeping open of the drains and dykes has prevented the growth of bushes and deciduous trees which are a feature of fens in their natural state.

Medieval Reclamation in South Lincolnshire

In south Lincolnshire, an entirely different story emerges. The silt ridge which runs parallel to the coast was first settled by Germanic tribes during the seventh century, the name Holland given to this part of Lincoln-shire deriving from an Old English word meaning 'the highland' (it has nothing to do with the Netherlands or with the Old English word for 'a hollow' from which the name Holbeach is derived.) The villages in which they settled lie on a line from Tydd St Mary and Lutton on the west bank of the Ouse—Nene estuary, as far as Wain-fleet and include Holbeach, Spalding, Donington, Kirton, Skirbeck, Wrangle and many others. Not all these place names are of Germanic origin as some of the later settlers were Danish, more particularly north of the one-time inlet of Bicker Haven. A survival from this period is the Elloe stone [TF 316248], the meeting place of the inhabitants of parishes to the south of the Wash which comprised the wapentake of Elloe.

The villages on this southernmost silt ridge prospered and the population grew to such an extent that the area of land between sea and fen became insufficient to meet its needs. About 1100 the villagers responded by starting to reclaim land beyond the sea banks, the work going

35

forward in stages, often involving co-operation between neighbouring communities, until the so-called 'Roman' bank was established in the late thirteenth century. This bank, which owes nothing to the Romans, marked the limit of seaward reclamation until the reign of Charles II. Many remains of this sea bank are visible today to the searcher armed with a one-inch Ordnance Survey map. Generally speaking, the bank is easiest to trace where a road runs along it and least prominent where it crosses cultivated fields.

On the fenward side of the silt ridge, the reclamation began later (about 1150) but proceeded more rapidly so that during the space of a hundred years about 50 square miles of fenland were reclaimed between the estuaries of the Ouse–Nene and the Welland. Many of the banks can be traced today: from the line of the pre-Norman Austendyke, followed today by the B1165 road, the reclamation proceeded to Saturday Dyke (1160–70); Hassock Dyke and the old Fendyke of Sutton (1190–95); Asgardyke, the course of which is partly that of the eighteenth-century South Holland Main Drain (1206); and as far as the Asendyke and Common Dyke (1241).

The result of these and later seaward reclamations is a series of parishes which are among the most elongated in England, being 12 to 17 miles long in the north-south direction and only two or three miles wide. Wide grassy droves along the spine of each parish provided a means of communication between the original townships and the hamlets established on the reclaimed land at Whaplode Drove, Holbeach Drove, Gedney Hill and Sutton St Edmund.

These reclamations brought the parishes to the boundaries of the Precinct of Crowland and there then ensued one of the most famous of medieval lawsuits in order to determine the common rights on the marsh, now that the villagers had transformed their own marshes into 'good and fertile ploughland'. The decision, which went against the men of Holland, did not endear King John to them and the true cause of his death after spending a night at Swineshead Abbey in 1216 remains uncertain to this day!

Similar reclamations took place further north in the wapentakes of Kirton, between Spalding and Boston, and of Skirbeck, between Boston and Wrangle and beyond as far as Wainfleet.

In Kirton, sections of a sea bank, parts of which are thought to have been built before the Norman conquest, can be traced round the head of Bicker Haven and thence between the villages of Fosdyke and Wyberton. Two banks can be traced on the fenward side: the Old Fendyke which ran northward from the A151 road just west of Spalding [TF 219220] to Donington where it joined the banks round the head of Bicker Haven, and the New Fendyke, further west, which started from Pode Hole and swept round the head of the former estuary, following the line of the Old Hammond Beck towards Boston. The dates of these banks are uncertain, but the New Fendyke is known to have been completed before 1179.

In Skirbeck and further north, there was once again reclamation from both sea and fen. The earliest sea bank, probably of Germanic or Danish origin, followed the line of Leverton Highgate and of the road and raised footpath that runs north-east from Wrangle Hall, parallel to the modern A52 road, to the Steeping River at Wainfleet All Saints. Outside this bank there were many salterns at the time of Domesday (1086): 41 at Leake Floors (TF 424488) and others at Wrangle Tofts, Friskney Tofts and Wainfleet Tofts (TF 495573). These salterns were man-made banks from which the salt-saturated sand was removed to make a salt solution which was then allowed to evaporate in shallow pans; those at Wainfleet Tofts are plainly visible today. Again the date of the medieval sea bank is uncertain. In the course of these reclamations, the havens at Fishtoft,

Freiston, Leake and Wrangle were either reduced in size or eliminated altogether.

There were two fen banks. The earlier one, known as the Ing Dyke and the Old Fendyke, is still mostly a fen bank; it follows the winding road from Hilldyke (TF 343476), by way of Leake Common Side, the grange of Waltham Abbey at King's Hill, and Friskney to the boundary of Wainfleet All Saints.

During the twelfth and thirteenth centuries, reclamation was also taking place on the northern and western edges of the Lincolnshire fens. From Burgh-le-Marsh in the east to Tattershall in the west, the communities on the southern edges of the wolds were draining and enclosing the fenlands to the south of them, establishing colonies in a pattern similar to those on the siltlands around the coast; the advance from Toynton All Saints, to Toynton St Peter, then to Toynton Fen Side and finally to Toynton Ings was typical of this colonisation. Other enclosures were taking place on either side of the gravel ridge which extends from Sibsey to Stickford and divides East Fen from West Fen. The medieval Northdyke Causeway along this ridge is today the course of the A16 trunk road, and although its highest point is actually only 28ft above sea level, it seems to the traveller to be much higher.

The communities lying along the line of the Car Dyke between Lincoln and Market Deeping also began draining and enclosing the fenland on their eastern borders shortly after the Norman conquest, though the main enclosure did not occur until the twelfth and thirteenth centuries.

Thus in Lincolnshire alone, by the year 1300, over 100 square miles of fertile ground had been reclaimed from sea and fen as a result of the activities of the inhabitants of individual parishes. In many cases they no doubt collaborated with their neighbours on either side, but there was no overall plan of any kind.

The maintenance and repair of banks and ditches was a local responsibility, often tied to the ownership or lease of a particular piece of land. Inevitably there were defaulters, and since one defaulter was enough to cause a flood, floods were frequent. It was often difficult to determine who was responsible for the upkeep of a particular section of bank and many long disputes resulted.

Eventually, in 1258, the central government was forced to intervene. This it did by appointing Commissions of Sewers, courts established to determine responsibilities and to ensure their fulfilment. Their function was to see that existing works were kept in repair rather than to initiate the construction of new ones. There were however exceptions: for example, a decision by a Court of Sewers in 1422 led to the construction of the New Podyke, when the foundations of the Old Podyke were found to be too weak to justify further repairs.

The Podyke was the bank on the southern edge of the Norfolk Marshland, that area of silt lying between the estuaries at Wisbech and Lynn. It was surrounded on all sides by sea, river or fen and was effectively an island until the first bridges were constructed in the nineteenth century. In spite of the bank around its perimeter and the many drains within it, it was subject to frequent flooding by the sea in medieval times, no fewer than twelve such occasions being recorded between the years 1250 and 1350. Yet, it was one of the wealthiest parts of England at that time as the land was ideally suited to sheep rearing. Its splendid parish churches bear witness to this wealth as we shall see in a later chapter.

It was during this period that the silting up of the Wisbech outfall caused the waters of the river Ouse to find their exit to the sea at Lynn; in some cases this added 50 miles to their journey and so reduced even more the slope of the rivers. The estuary at Lynn also began to silt up as the slow-running rivers were unable to carry away the silt deposited by the flood—it became shallow and wide, sometimes as much as a mile across.

Purely local action could not prevent the estuaries silting up and the time was undoubtedly ripe for the initiation of larger works, of a kind which had not been undertaken since the departure of the Romans, over a thousand years before.

Bishop Morton of Ely was the first person to carry through such a work. He created Morton's Leam, a cut 12 miles long, 40ft wide and 4ft deep, to carry the waters of the river Nene direct from near Peterborough to Guyhirne instead of allowing them to follow a longer, roundabout route to the south. Bishop Morton's work of about 1490 was followed by other isolated efforts carried through by villages or individual landowners: the Maud Foster drain was cut in 1568 to drain the land north of Boston and to carry the water into the river Witham at a sluice just below the town; Sir John Popham made an attempt, which was later abandoned, to drain the land around Upwell in 1605, cutting the drain known as Popham's Eau from the Nene to Nordelph on the Well Creek.

The Draining of the Bedford Level

Although a climate of opinion in favour of a general draining was developing, there was very great opposition from the fenmen themselves and considerable difficulties. The fens were far from being unproductive in their marshy state and the fenmen feared the loss of the supplies of fish, fowl, turf and reed which were readily available to them. Moreover there was opposition from those who feared the disturbance to established waterways; it was even suggested officially that the colleges of Cambridge might have to be abandoned owing to lack of provisions in the town!

Another difficulty was the lack of capital. The

commoners were poor and there were few large estates in the Fenland. Only by attracting adventurers who were willing to risk their capital in return for a part of the land when drained, was such a project made possible.

A General Draining Act had been passed in 1600 but it was another thirty years before work was started on any comprehensive undertaking to drain the 400,000 acres of the southern fenlands. Then in 1630, fourteen adventurers, including the fourth Earl of Bedford as undertaker, committed themselves to the project and appointed a Dutchman, Cornelius Vermuyden, as engineer. The fenmen were suspicious of all foreigners and did not welcome Vermuyden, notwithstanding the experience he had acquired in draining Hatfield Chase in south Yorkshire, a work for which he was knighted.

Vermuyden recognised that new straight channels must be cut to carry away the waters by as steep a route as could be obtained in so flat a district. The rivers flowing through the Fenland drain an area roughly four times that of the Fenland itself and the water runs comparatively rapidly off the high ground into the Fenland basin and accumulates there until it can escape to the sea. Sluices were to be built to prevent inundation by exceptional high tides in the sea.

On the Great Ouse, Vermuyden cut the Bedford river from Earith to Salter's Lode, a drain 21 miles long and 70ft wide with a sluice at each end. On the Nene, Morton's Leam was remade and the Horseshoe sluice built below Wisbech. New South Eau, Shire Drain, Peakirk Drain, Bevill's Leam and Sam's Cut were cut or remade to provide channels for water to escape into the main rivers from the fens on the edge of the high ground.

The result of several years work and the expenditure of over £100,000 was the conversion of marsh into 'summer grounds'—land that was dry in summer but which was not immune from flooding during the winter.

Some of the adventurers were virtually bankrupt by this time and King Charles I took it upon himself to complete the work and convert the 'summer grounds' into 'winter grounds'—land immune from floods throughout the year.

At this stage, the Civil War broke out and in the ensuing confusion opponents of the draining wrought much damage to the works. During the Commonwealth, in 1649, a further Act was passed and the fifth Earl of Bedford was appointed undertaker, with Vermuyden once more as engineer.

The largest work carried out during this second period was the cutting of the New Bedford river or Hundred Foot Drain. This runs roughly parallel to the Old Bedford river, but with a space between the two rivers about half a mile wide to act as a reservoir in which surplus water could accumulate in time of flood; today this area, the Ouse Washes, is an important nature reserve (see Chapter 11). The New Bedford river became the main channel for the waters of the river Ouse and its former course via Ely was cut off by Hermitage Sluice at Earith at the south and by Denver Sluice at the north end, St John's Eau being cut to make it possible to convey flood water from the South Level (that is the Ely Ouse and its tributaries) into the river at Stowbridge five miles below Denver.

In the Middle Level, the area between the Bedford rivers and Morton's Leam, the Forty Foot or Vermuyden's Drain was cut from Ramsey to Welches Dam on the Old Bedford river, and Popham's Eau resuscitated, to link the Old Nene with the Ouse. Other drains built in the Middle Level included the Twenty Foot river near March, the Sixteen Foot Drain to the west of the Bedford rivers and roughly parallel to them, and Tongs Drain which acted as a further relief channel in the Denver area. Besides drains, banks and sluices, many roads and bridges were built.

The work was judged to have been completed in 1652 and a few years later, after the restoration of the monarchy, a board was established to maintain the works, with power to raise money by taxes on the 95,000 acres of the adventurers' land.

Thus was concluded the first act in the great drama of the southern Fenland. Not all the works that Vermuyden had proposed were carried out and another three centuries were to elapse before his full plans for draining the South Level were implemented. Vermuyden himself left the Fens in 1655 and little is known of his subsequent life. He was harshly judged by his contemporaries and for many years afterwards, but the fact remains that he carried through a vast scheme in the face of great opposition and that his works constitute the backbone of the modern drainage of the 'Great Level of the Fens'.

The Eighteenth Century

For a few years all was well. Land was brought under cultivation which a few years before had been marsh. Crops of flax, hemp, oats, wheat, cole-seed and woad were grown and there was an increase in the number of cows and sheep. The meres and lakes, which had been excluded from the draining, continued to provide fish and fowl in abundance.

But trouble lay ahead. Many of the old problems remained: in spite of the shortened rivers, their flow was still much weaker than that of the tides and silt continued to build up not only in the estuaries but also in front of Denver Sluice. Denver was a crisis point as within a short distance the Ouse, now diverted down the New Bedford river, received the waters of the Ely Ouse, of the drains leading into the Old Bedford river and of Well Creek. Moreover, a combination of high tides and heavy rain in the upland areas could raise the level of the water in the New Bedford river so much that none of the sluice gates leading into it could be opened; flood waters built up behind the sluices and navigation through Denver ceased, often for several days at a time.

The greatest problems had not been foreseen at all; they arose from the nature of the topsoil. Throughout the drained area this was peat, a sponge-like substance formed from the decayed vegetation, capable of absorbing large amounts of water when submerged, but which shrank and lost its strength when dried. The effect of the drainage therefore was a general lowering in the level of the land: thus land which was about 12ft above Ordnance Datum when first drained has now sunk to within one or two feet of OD. In such a situation, draining by gravity became impossible and 'engines' had to be employed to lift the water from the field drains into the feeder drains, and thence into the main drains. The other effect of the drying out of the peat was to weaken the banks, which had to be rebuilt with clay and other stronger but much less readily available materials.

At first there was severe opposition to the use of engines which it was felt interfered with the drainage as a whole and tended to drain one area at the expense of another. This was the result of lack of an overall plan, a situation which led during the eighteenth century to the establishment of internal drainage boards to organise and maintain the drains and engines in each local district. The engines were originally either horse-mills or windmills and it is known that some were in use before 1600.

Floods once more became frequent as the Bedford Level Corporation, with inadequate funds, struggled to repair its banks and scour its drains. Disaster struck in 1713 when Denver Sluice was destroyed and the silting that had occurred below the site of the sluice caused the water from the Bedford river to flow up the Ely Ouse instead of continuing on its course towards the sea. Thirty-five years of argument and counter-argument were to elapse before a start was made on rebuilding the sluice.

There were few new works in the southern Fenland

during the eighteenth century. Most of the area between the river Cam and the fen-edge villages of Burwell, Swaffham and Bottisham was drained in 1766. Smith's Leam was cut in 1728 to carry the Nene from Peterborough to Guyhirne and attempts were made to confine the Nene outfall to a single narrow channel below Wisbech instead of allowing it to meander through the marshes. These attempts were at first opposed by the town but after four successive inundations between 1763 and 1770 and many years of impeded navigation, Kindersley's Cut was built; it had an immediate beneficial effect on the drainage of the North Level, demonstrating once again the importance of providing satisfactory outfalls for the rivers.

Above all, though, the eighteenth century was the century of the windmill. Hundreds of them were in use, sometimes operating in pairs to provide a double lift, and wherever one went in the Fenland, ten, twenty, thirty or even forty could be seen across the levels. What a sight it must have been when a moderate wind was blowing!

To complete the story up to the end of the eighteenth century, we must look at what had been happening in the Lincolnshire fens since the General Draining Act was passed in 1600. The local reclamations during the twelfth and thirteenth centuries (p 35) had left many areas of fen undrained and, with so much activity elsewhere, it was inevitable that proposals to drain these areas should have been put forward in the seventeenth century. There was no overall scheme comparable to that carried out in the southern fens and such success as there was, was mainly short-lived.

Two separate efforts were made to drain Deeping Fen before the Civil War, but it was only after a further effort following an Act of 1666 that some success was achieved. Attempts to drain East Fen, West Fen and Wildmore Fen, to the north and east of the river Witham, yielded only temporary success and the works were thrown down by the dispossessed fenmen during the Civil War and not repaired afterwards. A similar story could be told of the Earl of Lindsey's draining of South Holland Fen, to the south and west of Boston, a work which involved the cutting of the South Forty Foot Drain from the river Glen near Bourne to Boston.

So things remained until the middle of the eighteenth century, by which time the condition of the northern fens had reverted to a state little different from that of 150 years earlier. New drainage works were then put in hand and considerable areas of land were freed from water, at least for the greater part of each year.

In Deeping Fen, which was peat, windmills were introduced to counteract the effects of the lowered land surface—over 50 were at work by 1763 in this one fen—new sluices were built and channels enlarged. On the siltlands between the Nene and the Welland, the pattern of the twelfth and thirteenth centuries was repeated with each parish enclosing new lands from both sea and fen; to integrate the drainage the South Holland Main Drain was cut in 1793–6.

Action in North Holland, south of the Witham, was stimulated by the very severe floods of 1763: old sluices and drains were restored and improved, and the Black Sluice erected where the South Forty Foot Drain entered the river Witham.

The draining of the Witham Fens, which lay to the north-east of Boston and extended almost to Lincoln, was motivated partly by a desire to improve navigation on the river Witham. The cutting of the North Forty Foot Drain in 1720 by Earl Fitzwilliam had not proved effective and it was later necessary to embank the land and to introduce windmills to remove the unwanted water. The Grand Sluice at Boston, completed in 1766, formed part of this scheme.

The Grand Sluice was not the first sluice to have been built across the river Witham at Boston. The report of a commission during the reign of Henry VII had led to the appointment of a certain May Hake, probably a Dutch-man, to construct a sluice to prevent seawater flowing up the river above Boston. Although the associated bridge remained in use until 1807, the sluice gates are known to have been removed before 1642.

The Nineteenth Century

The nineteenth century saw a succession of distinguished engineers grappling with the problems of fen drainage. Smeaton had been consulted some years earlier but the works he advocated were never built owing to lack of funds. Indeed, the same fate awaited many of the proposals subsequently put forward by John Rennie, his son Sir John Rennie, Telford and many others whose names are less well known.

Nevertheless much was achieved. In particular a determined effort was made to improve the outfalls of the four rivers, reliable steam engines replaced the uncertain windmills for lifting water out of the drains into the rivers, and those parts of the Fenland where there had hitherto been virtually no effective drainage, were cleared of water, at least until the surface sank to create new difficulties.

On the Great Ouse, the Eau Brink Cut was completed in 1821 between St Germans and King's Lynn in order to confine the river to a deep straight channel instead of allowing it to take a much longer course among shifting sandbanks to the west. This cut was extended seawards by the Norfolk Estuary Company in 1853, with training banks built in the Wash itself, as part of a scheme to reclaim land from the sea.

The Nene estuary had deteriorated to such an extent that only quite small ships could reach Wisbech, larger ones having to load and unload under exposed conditions at Sutton Wash. Reports by both Rennie and Telford stressed the need for a new straight channel from Wisbech to the Wash at Crab Hole and eventually, after much argument and counter-argument, this was built. It was combined with a scheme for building an embankment and road from Walpole Cross Keys to Sutton Bridge and the erection of a bridge there. The present swing bridge is the third on this site and was built in 1894–7 to replace one built by Robert Stephenson in 1850. However, the river through Wisbech itself remained narrow and tortuous and continued to present an obstacle to shipping and to the free flow and ebb of the tidal water.

In reporting on the equally dismal state of affairs in the Welland estuary, James Walker (who attributed the suggestion to Mr Beasley), proposed a comparatively simple and inexpensive way of building training walls, which was subsequently adopted for all similar works in the estuaries of the Fenland rivers. In this, the walls are built up from thorn faggots weighted with clay, the branches of which interlock; the interstices fill with silt carried up by the tide to give a solid embankment up to half-tide level. One and a half miles below Fosdyke were so treated in 1838 and there was a temporary improvement. However, the funds available to the Welland Trustees were inadequate to extend the training walls or to maintain those that were built and flooding in the interior was frequent throughout the nineteenth century.

The engineers who reported on the state of affairs in the Witham outfall all condemned the Grand Sluice and advocated the building of an improved channel below Boston. The channel as far as Hobhole Sluice was improved in 1841 and a new cut made from there to the Wash at Clayhole in 1884. Access to Boston docks was greatly improved by these works, but floods in the Witham valley above the Grand Sluice continued to be a frequent occurrence.

The beneficial effect on the general drainage brought about by the lowering of the river beds at their outfalls was supplemented by several new works in the interior of the Fenland. In the South Level, the river Ouse was straightened from Ely to Littleport Bridge and a number of new sluices built and old ones, including Denver Sluice, were reconstructed.

Considerable attention was paid to improving the drainage of the Middle Level. Several schemes were proposed and the one actually adopted in 1843 combined parts from each one; it centred around the construction of the Middle Level Main Drain from the Sixteen Foot river near Upwell direct to the Ouse at St Germans and the draining of Whittlesey Mere, which was by 1851 the last remaining large area of water in the Fenland and a potential danger to the lower-lying land to the north and east of it.

The sluice at St Germans, through which the Middle Level Drain discharges into the Ouse, has had an unhappy history. It was destroyed in 1862, causing extensive flooding in the Norfolk Marshland. The dam and siphons which replaced it proved unsatisfactory and a larger sluice had to be built in 1880. Ultimately it was realised that gravity drainage on its own was insufficient to keep the Middle Level clear of water in times of flood and, in 1934, powerful pumps were installed.

The lowering of the river bed in the Nene outfall at Gunthorpe Sluice had an immediate effect on the drainage of the North Level and this was improved further by the construction of the North Level Main Drain in 1831–4. So successful were these works that they made redundant two of the earliest steam pumping engines to be installed in the Fens, those at Sutton St Edmund and Borough Fen!

John Rennie had recommended the installation of a steam engine in 1789 for draining Soham and Bottisham Fens, but it was not until 1817 that the first such engine was actually installed: a 12hp engine at Sutton St Edmund. The steam engine had two enormous advantages over the windmill: it could work at all times and not just when a wind of the right strength was blowing, and it had much greater reserves of power.

The first engine to be installed in the southern Fens was the Ten Mile Bank engine of 1819. Apart from the fact that it had two scoop wheels, it was typical of those which bore the brunt of the work of fen drainage for the next 100 years. By the middle of the century over 50 engines were at work, the largest having a nominal output of 80hp and capable of draining an area of 8–10,000 acres, roughly ten times that with which a windmill could cope under ideal conditions.

The replacement of the windmill by the steam engine led to changes in the pattern of drains. Minor drains now led into larger ones, called 'engine drains' or 'commissioners drains', from which the water was pumped into the rivers. Engine drains are sometimes straight or they may zig-zag through the area they serve, occasionally passing under channels at a higher level.

Whittlesey Mere, an area of well over 1,000 acres of water, was not the only part of the Fenland to be made into productive farmland during the nineteenth century. Earlier, John Rennie had drawn up a plan for draining the three fens to the north of Boston. East Fen was to be drained by a new channel to the Witham at Hobhole Sluice, and Wildmore Fen and West Fen by a channel leading to Maud Foster Sluice, Boston. In addition, a catchwater drain along the northern edge of the three fens was intended to carry water from the Wolds into the Witham at Maud Foster Sluice.

This plan was carried out successfully, but as the peat shrank conditions deteriorated and steam engines had to be installed. The building of the new cut from Hobhole Sluice to the Wash at Clayhole in 1884 also had a beneficial effect on the drainage of the three fens.

The work of reclaiming land from the Wash continued throughout the nineteenth century and is still going on today. Many thousands of acres of farmland have been won as a result of this steady but unexciting work.

The Twentieth Century

To us, it seems incredible that through almost three centuries of floods and disasters no public bodies existed to tackle the problems of fen drainage as a whole in each catchment area or had the power to co-ordinate the activities of the various internal drainage authorities. Yet, such was the strength of local independence that not until the passing of the Land Drainage Act in 1930 was this chaotic situation remedied. The catchment boards established then were subsequently replaced, in the Fens, by three river authorities responsible for the Great Ouse, the Welland and Nene, and Lincolnshire. All three bodies are now divisions of the Anglian Water Authority.

After 1930, it became possible, for the first time, to carry out scientific investigations into the causes of flooding and the relative merits of particular remedies. An experimental model of the Wash and the tidal part of the Great Ouse was constructed at Cambridge to provide data on tidal and silting conditions. At the time at which it was constructed, this model was the largest of its kind in the world, occupying a shed 75ft by 55ft. To model the river, extensive surveys had to be made in the Wash and it was necessary to measure the cross-section of the river every quarter mile from the sea as far upstream as Brownshill Staunch.

The urgency of the work was brought home by floods in 1936 and again in the following year, when the water was at bank top height in the Ouse Washes for many miles and the situation was critical for nearly two weeks.

To sort out the conflicting views about what should be done, the consulting engineers, Sir Murdoch MacDonald and Partners, were brought in. Their report advocated the building of the Cut-off Channel round the eastern edge of the fens, which by intercepting the waters of the Lark, Little Ouse and Wissey is able to reduce by 40 per cent the flood discharge reaching Denver Sluice from the South Level. To carry the flood discharges from the Cut-off Channel and the Ely Ouse away from Denver, the Relief Channel has been built, roughly parallel to the tidal river, almost to King's Lynn. This channel is sufficiently wide and deep to contain the whole of the flood discharge during the period that the automatic sluice gates at King's Lynn are closed against an incoming tide and then to discharge it, together with the full flood flow, before the next high tide.

The implementation of these plans was delayed by World War II and, before they could be carried out, the Fens suffered the greatest flood of which there is any record. In March 1947 there were major inundations in the South Level (37,000 acres flooded), near Crowland (20,000 acres flooded) and in Lincoln. Furthermore, the highest recorded tidal surge in the North Sea occurred six years later, flooding parts of King's Lynn and breaching the banks between King's Lynn and Denver. Both these experiences led to modifications of the South Level scheme as it was eventually carried out.

A cut-off channel, following a somewhat similar course to that actually built, and a shorter relief channel had formed part of Vermuyden's original proposals. It is tragic that three centuries were allowed to elapse before the plans of this far-sighted and much maligned engineer were vindicated. Sir John Rennie, too, had advocated the construction of a cut-off channel.

These major works in the South Level were accompanied by a widening and deepening of the Ely Ouse from its junction with the Cam to Denver, by a general heightening and strengthening of the flood banks, by works in the Wash intended to keep open the shipping channels and by improvements in the internal drainage districts.

The powerful pumping station installed at St Germans in 1934 has not solved all the problems of drainage in the Middle Level since the depth of the peat, and its subsequent shrinkage, far away in Holme Fen is so great that the surface is below Ordnance Datum there. To get water to flow from Holme Fen to St Germans by gravity would involve deepening and widening the drains to such an extent that many acres of highly productive farmland would be lost. Consequently, it was decided instead to install additional pumping stations at Mount Pleasant and Pondersbridge. Thus some water from the Holme Fen area has to be triple pumped before it reaches the sea: first into a main drain, then boosted at either Mount Pleasant or Pondersbridge according to the route it follows, and finally pumped into the Ouse at St Germans.

Although the works undertaken by the River Nene Catchment Board may not have been so spectacular, its achievements during its 20 years of existence were equally remarkable. When the Board was formed, the upper Nene was in a deplorable state: the locks were decayed and whole sections of the river were choked with weeds, reeds, mud and silt, so that flooding was frequent. Lower down, there were shoals of hard gravel in the river bed, the banks were collapsing in many places and there was silting in the estuary.

The Board's major work was the construction of Dog-in-a-Doublet sluices and lock, five miles below Peterborough, which then became the upper limit of the tidal river. Besides protecting the river above the sluices from tidal surges, they also helped to conserve water upstream in times of drought and to ensure that there was an adequate depth of water through Peterborough.

The course of the river through Wisbech received particular attention. Since the proximity of roads and buildings prevented widening of the river, piles had to be used to contain the banks for a distance of two miles. At the same time, the town quay was rebuilt. One result of all this activity was to make it possible for small coasters to navigate upstream as far as Peterborough.

The Nene Catchment Board was the first one in Britain to install a complete system for gauging and measuring the flow in the river throughout its length—an achievement which led Sir William Beach Thomas to describe the Nene at the time as 'the most scientifically managed . . . of all our rivers'.

As at St Germans on the Ouse, so at the point at which the North Level Main Drain enters the Nene, gravity drainage became insufficient and a pumping station had to be installed. During the 1947 floods, the pumps, which could handle 10¾ million gallons of water an hour, ran for seven weeks non-stop!

Plans for a major improvement scheme for the river Welland had been drawn up in 1944, but in the aftermath of the war their implementation was too late to prevent the disastrous floods at Crowland in 1947, though it is hoped that they will prevent a repetition of them.

The river has been widened and deepened throughout its length from Uffington to the sea. This involved the building of three new cuts: the Coronation Channel which bypasses Spalding, through which the existing channel is hemmed in by roads and buildings, the Maxey Cut which provides a direct channel for the automatic discharge of floodwater which might otherwise cause flooding in the Deeping area, and the Greatford Cut which can be used to divert flood waters from the river Glen into the improved river Welland below the Deepings. The building of these cuts involved the construction of several new sluices and bridges and the reconstruction of existing ones. Many miles of floodbanks have been built up and strengthened so that Cowbit and Crowland washes can be used as reservoirs to relieve pressure on the banks elsewhere.

In the Witham fens during the past 50 years, the story has been one of steady improvement rather than of major development, particular examples being the comprehensive scheme undertaken in the area to the south-west of Boston drained by the South Forty Foot Drain which discharges into the Witham at the Black Sluice Pumping Station, and the cutting of a relief channel from Thorpe Culvert to the Steeping river at Haven House and the building of the tidal sluices at Wainfleet Clough on the northern boundary of the Fens.

Conclusion

There are now, in effect, two separate but inter-dependent drainage systems in the Fenland. The rivers, embanked above the level of the surrounding land, carry the water which descends from the higher ground around the fens and take it to the sea. The internal drainage system collects the rainwater that falls on the fens themselves and feeds it into main drains, which in turn discharge into the rivers. Such water has to be lifted once, sometimes twice and occasionally three times. For this task, diesel-driven pumps have replaced the steam pumping engines, and are now being increasingly replaced by automatically-operated electric plants.

In a country that is becoming short of water, it is not surprising that the possibility of making more positive use of the surplus water that flows through the Fenland is being investigated. Already a major scheme has been implemented for transferring water by tunnel and pipe-line to the headwaters of the rivers Stour and Black-water in Essex, which feed reservoirs at Abberton and Hanningfield respectively. When this is in operation, the Cut-off Channel is used to carry water from the Ely Ouse river system at Denver in reverse direction to the intake at Blackdyke.

A much more grandiose proposal to build freshwater storage reservoirs in the Wash, has been the subject of a major feasibility study, which itself cost over

£2,500,000. In the meantime, the Great Ouse River Division is pressing ahead with a scheme for the controlled extraction of water from boreholes in the chalk hills to the east of the fens. This is intended to suppress the discharge through natural springs, so that the water is available underground for extraction by pumping at times of the year when it is most needed, either by consumers or to supplement the flow in the river system. A pilot scheme carried out near the headwaters of the Little Ouse in 1968–71 showed that such a scheme was both possible and economic.

It has taken over 300 years to drain the fens and to provide really effective protection against flooding in all except the most adverse combination of circumstances. Today, it can be said that the Fens are among the best drained areas in the whole of Britain, but they will only remain so if the works are kept in constant repair and new ones undertaken as the need arises. As food prices rise, the cost of draining this large area of first class arable land can be borne by the crops it produces. Administrative complications and inadequate technology are no longer obstacles to effective drainage; only the stupidity and selfishness of man can undo the achievements of three centuries.

4 Waterways for Trade and Pleasure

DURING the centuries that preceded the building of railways and the application of the internal combustion engine to land transport, boats provided the main means of moving goods from one part of the Fenland to another. On the drier ground of the silt fens and in the peat fens after the general draining, people were able to travel on horseback but the state of the roads did not encourage the use of wheeled vehicles.

Early History

There is archaeological evidence of trade with other parts of Britain and countries overseas as early as the Bronze Age, and the Fenland waterways, even at that time, offered a ready means of entry into Britain for foreign invaders. Also the inhabitants of the Fenland and its peripheral settlements, in prehistoric as in medieval times, must have travelled by boat in their expeditions in search of fish and fowl, of reed for thatching and of turf for fuel.

The earliest boats of which we have any knowledge were canoes hewn out of the trunks of oak trees. A survey made by Sir Cyril Fox in 1926 (*Antiquaries Journal* 6, 121-51) lists nine from the Fens but a later writer (Thompson, *Lincs Architectural and Archaeological Society Reports and Papers* 5, 78) states that no fewer than eighteen have been found along the middle reach of the Witham alone. Yet only two Fenland examples survive in museums and, of these, only the one at Lincoln is of known origin.

Such boats have been dated from at least the early Bronze Age right up to the Christian era. One of the largest and most highly developed was found in Deeping Fen. It was 46ft long, with a maximum beam of 5ft 8in, and had a ribbed floor and an external keel cut out of the solid wood.

There is, however, no evidence that these prehistoric inhabitants of the Fenland did more than make use of such waterways as nature had provided. With the coming of the Romans, this changed and a determined effort was made to improve the lines of communication. Their most ambitious venture was the Car Dyke. Its course can be traced today from its junction with the Witham near Lincoln to Peterborough, and, further south, from the Old West River to Waterbeach.

The two sections of the Car Dyke and the canals between them (Coln Ditch and Cnut's Dyke) are thought to have formed part of a transport system built to carry supplies from East Anglia to the Roman armies in the north, the main cargoes being corn, wool for uniforms, leather for tents and shields, and salted meat. The system provided continuous inland water transport from Cambridge to York since a contemporary canal, the Fossdyke, linked the rivers Witham and Trent. A branch canal between Bourne and Morton is interesting in that there is evidence of the existence of soak ditches parallel to the canal to take the water from the field ditches and discharge it into the canal.

We know that Reach Slade, just to the south-west of the present Reach Lode, is the silted-up course of a Roman canal. It connected the river Cam at Upware with the port of Reach, which would have been a natural loading point for the agricultural products of East Anglia on their way to the north. Another Roman waterway was the now extinct Rodham Farm Canal, north-east of March.

Beyond those, there is no certainty as to which of the artificial waterways in the Fens may have been built by the Romans and which may have been of later construction. What is certain is that almost all the waterways that exist today are artificial. They are too straight to be natural in such flat country, and, in many cases, the previous winding course of a river is plainly visible in the nearby fields as a roddon, or is indicated by differences in the colour of the soil or by crop marks. Some waterways cut through islands or peninsulas of mineral soil and in places their direction runs across that of the natural drainage of a district; such waterways can only be artificial.

Historical records enable us to date most of the waterways which have been dug since the Norman conquest, but there remain a great many of which the origin is still unknown. When were these built, and why?

Medieval River Traffic

Throughout the medieval period, the waterways remained the highways of the fen country. There were further unwelcome incursions of water-borne invaders and the devastation wrought to the abbeys by raiding parties of Danes about AD 870 is described in Chapter 5. With their shallow draught, the Danish longships were able to penetrate right into the heart of Britain, as the remains of a Danish fortress and docks on the upper Ouse at Willington, just below Bedford, testify.

Building materials en route to Fenland abbeys and churches became an increasingly important cargo. Stone from the quarries at Barnack, between Peterborough and Stamford, was used in Cambridge (St Bene'ts church), Ramsey, Crowland and Spalding and in several churches in Norfolk and Suffolk, at least as early as the eleventh century. The traffic in stone increased enormously after the arrival of the Normans with their grandiose ecclesiastical and military building projects. Thus we find Barnack stone used in the abbeys at Ely, Norwich and Bury St Edmunds, for facing the Norman keep at Castle Hedingham in Essex, in Norman churches and, here and there, in some of the earliest college buildings in Cambridge (most Barnack stone now to be seen in Cambridge is actually re-used material from vandalised Fenland abbeys). So important was water transport to the monks building Sawtry Abbey in Huntingdonshire (TL 197826) that they dug a canal three miles long to connect their building site with the river system.

Others of the famous quarries on the limestone belt in the Stamford area were worked in the medieval period: Weldon, Ancaster, Ketton, Clipsham, King's Cliffe and Stamford itself. Later, we find stone from them used at important building sites many miles from the quarries, notably Clipsham stone at Windsor Castle c1360, Ancaster stone in medieval churches at Norwich and at Louth, King's Cliffe stone at Hengrave Hall in Suffolk and so on. Such journeys depended on the ready availability of water transport over a considerable distance. Gunwade Ferry on the river Nene, near Caistor, seems to have been an important loading point for stone from the southern group of quarries and the river Slea provided an outlet for stone from Ancaster.

The medieval fairs generated much traffic on the Fenland rivers. These gatherings for large-scale trading were held annually, generally in the late summer or early autumn, and some were of sufficient importance to attract merchants from overseas. The fairs at St Ives, Boston and Stamford were of international stature during the reign of King John and later Stourbridge fair, held on a meadow just outside Cambridge, eclipsed them all in importance. Although particular fairs had a reputation for dealing in particular products, at any of the larger ones, wool, hops, grain, horses, sheep, cattle, dairy produce, salt, agricultural implements and other manufactured goods were bought and sold.

Much of this produce travelled by waterway and so did many of the merchants attending the fairs. It would hardly have been possible in medieval times to hold a great fair which was far removed from water communication. The Fenland rivers with their lack of tolls and absence of weirs, mills and other impediments in their lower reaches encouraged such commerce, as it did the lesser business transacted at regular weekly markets in the smaller towns.

By the later Middle Ages, a considerable amount of the trade of the Fenland was with overseas. Boston rivalled Hull in being next in importance to London as the largest wool exporting port in England in 1350. A few years later, King's Lynn was constituted a staple port, while the warehouses of the Hanseatic League (which still survive) were established in the fifteenth century.

There was a reduction in traffic on the Fenland rivers following the dissolution of the monasteries in the sixteenth century. No longer was the surplus produce of monastic estates conveyed to fairs and markets, nor did sacrists and other monastic officers journey to their outlying estates; the transport of building materials was much reduced.

The Canalized Rivers

The reduction was only temporary however, for, about 1600, began the golden age of river transport in Britain. From then until about 1750 great efforts were made to improve the rivers and to use them as a means of communication. It was only after the rivers had been canalized, that the canals proper were built to complement them and to complete the system of inland waterways which existed before the railway age.

The Fenland was no exception to these developments. During the seventeenth and eighteenth centuries, Acts were passed to improve navigation on the Great Ouse as far as Bedford, on the Cam to Cambridge, on the Lark to Bury St Edmunds, on the Little Ouse to Thetford, on the Nar to Westacre, on the Nene to Northampton, on the Welland to Stamford, by the Bourne Eau and river Glen to Bourne, on the Witham to Lincoln and, by the Fossdyke, beyond Lincoln to the river Trent at Torksey. In addition, two routes through the Middle Level were made navigable: one from Salters Lode (TF 586015) via Outwell and Whittlesey Dyke to Stanground (TL 209973) and the other from the Old Bedford river to the Nene by way of the Forty Foot Drain. These improvements involved the construction of pound locks around the watermills which abounded in the upper reaches of the rivers and the building of staunches in order to raise the water level in the stretches of river immediately above them. Thus a staunch was built at St Ives to increase the depth of water through the town sufficiently to enable vessels to pass over the shallows by the bridge without grounding.

The general drainage of the southern Fens carried out in the middle of the seventeenth century had an immediate effect on navigation. The construction of the New Bedford river shortened the distance from Earith to Denver by ten miles, providing a straight deep channel between those two points while, on the other hand, the building of Denver Sluice impeded navigation on the Ely Ouse and its four tributaries (the Cam, Lark, Little Ouse and Wissey) and caused silting in the tidal river below Denver (see p 43). The first Denver sluice had no lock and the passage of boats through the sluice could be hazardous, if it was not prevented altogether by the gates which often had to be kept closed for long periods in winter to exclude the tides and in the summer to maintain the water level in the South Level.

All the Draining Acts required the Bedford Level Corporation to maintain the rights of navigation, but did not give the Corporation power to improve them or to collect tolls from the boat owners who continued to have the benefit of free navigation. Almost permanent conflict existed throughout the seventeenth, eighteenth and nineteenth centuries between the navigation and drainage interests, not only about the state of the rivers, but also over the damage done to the flood banks by the passage of towing horses.

Until the fens were drained, lighters were towed by gangs of men since the river banks were usually too soft to support the weight of horses. When the wind was favourable, a square sail could be set and towing became unnecessary. Quanting was another method of propulsion: a heavy pole known as a quant was dropped into the river from the bow of a vessel by a man who then walked aft, applying his weight to the pole to move the boat forward. The method was widely used on the Norfolk Broads before auxiliary engines were fitted in yachts and wherries.

The vessels which traded on the Fenland rivers while they were still tidal were of the type known as Humber Keels. Their bluff bows and long straight vertical sides gave them a large carrying capacity but made them rather inelegant. A single square sail was mounted amidships and leeboards were fitted to provide lateral resistance. A typical Keel was about 60ft long and 15ft

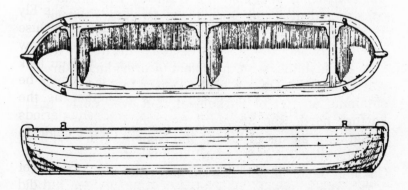

Fig 2 Elevation and plan of a Fenland Lighter
(*Drawn by Robert Wilson from plans by John K. Wilson*)

beam and could carry about 40 tons of cargo when loaded to draw 3ft of water. A model of such a vessel may be seen at the National Maritime Museum.

After the building of Denver and Earith sluices, the Keels were largely superseded by the smaller Fenland Lighters. Cargoes were then transhipped at King's Lynn and carried up river in gangs of seven to ten lighters, the first one of which might carry a single square sail. A typical Fenland Lighter (fig 2) has recently been raised from the river bed near Ely and is now at the Cambridge Museum of Technology. She is about 45ft long with a beam of just over 10ft and would have had a carrying capacity of about 25 tons. The construction is extremely solid, roughly every third frame being of iron.

The Fenland Punt is a smaller but generally similar vessel used in the Fenland as a general working boat and for eel fishing. Such vessels may still be found in odd corners of the Fenland and one is on display at the National Maritime Museum; she is about 18ft long and 5ft beam and was propelled by a 12ft quant.

When the canal age was at its height, numerous plans were put forward to join the Fenland rivers to the main canal system. The only such connection actually built ran from the Nene at Northampton to the Grand Junction Canal; it replaced a tramway which had been constructed over the same route ten years earlier, in 1805. One of the most ambitious proposals was for a canal to connect the Stort at Bishop's Stortford with the Cam at Clayhithe, with the object of providing a through waterway from London to the Wash; this got as far as obtaining an Act of Parliament, but was never built. Further north, the Stamford Junction Canal was projected as a means of linking the Nene and the Witham with the Welland at Stamford, and the Welland with the Oakham Canal; it, too, proved abortive.

The three canals that were actually built in the Fenland were all quite small. The Wisbech canal connected the Nene at Wisbech with the Old Nene and the Well Creek at Outwell. Since the canal could only be filled from the Nene on a high spring tide, heavy traffic through the locks at either end lowered the water level to such an extent as to make the canal almost unusable for part of each month.

The company which built the Horncastle canal, linking Horncastle with the Witham, had the distinguished naturalist, Sir Joseph Banks, as its first chairman. It survived from 1802 to 1885. The Sleaford Navigation, which obtained its Act in 1794, made navigable the Sleaford Mill Stream and the Kyme Eau to their junction with the Witham. Both canals were built as feeder canals to the Witham Navigation.

The coming of the railways did not kill the waterways immediately, as they remained competitive for a time by reducing their rates for the carriage of non-urgent freight: coal, bricks, timber, etc. But the reduced tolls were insufficient to maintain the locks and other works, which eventually fell into decay. Brave efforts were made to restore navigation on both the upper Ouse and the Lark towards the end of the nineteenth century using steam driven vessels, but they did not last long.

Regular traffic continued however on the Ely Ouse and the Cam until well into the twentieth century, with steam tugs towing strings of steel barges to and from local industrial sites: the fertiliser factory and brickyard at Burwell, the brick industry at Horningsea, the sugar-beet refineries at Ely and Wissington, the gasworks at Cambridge, and the clunch quarries at Burwell and Reach. For a time, too, there was traffic in coprolites, the phosphatised nodules of fossils found in seams on top of the gault clay and used as a fertiliser. Coal, and later oil, travelled by water to isolated pumping stations, inaccessible by road; this traffic has finally come to an end now that many of the smaller pumping stations have been converted to automatic electrical operation. The only present day commercial traffic is that connected with the maintenance of the sluices and river banks, carrying clay and equipment from the Anglian Water Authority's depot at Roswell Pits, near Ely.

Pleasure Boating

While commercial traffic is now virtually extinct, the growth of pleasure boating has been phenomenal. One of the earliest recorded cruises was that undertaken by the Earl of Orford and his fleet of nine boats, the log book of which was subsequently published under the title *Lord Orford's Voyage Round the Fens in 1774*. There are other early records of pleasure boating, particularly on Whittlesey Mere, which was the scene of regular regattas before it was drained in 1851.

The present vogue for pleasure boating really began towards the end of the nineteenth century when the first clubs were established on the Fenland rivers. The Cambridge University Cruising Club (founded in 1893) was holding regular races at Ely in 1897 and the following year the first two of a class of centre-board sloop-rigged sharpies were built for one-design racing. After holding races for several years on the stretch of water above Houghton Mill, the club returned to Ely in 1911 and remained there until World War II.

The Cam Sailing Club was founded in 1899 and two years later began holding regular races on its present waters at Clayhithe. A team race held at Denver in 1902 against the Ouse Amateur Sailing Club, which must by then have been established at King's Lynn, is believed to have been one of the first inter-club matches sailed in Britain.

The power boats of that period were of course steam-driven but the formation of the Cambridge Motor Boat Club in 1913 carries the implication that the much more convenient—if, at first, less reliable—internal combustion engine was by then replacing steam as the motive power.

Great changes followed the end of the war in 1945.

Plate 4 (above) The superb Jacobean screen across the western end of the nave at Walpole St Peter, with the Perpendicular east window and the Jacobean pulpit beyond (*East Anglia Tourist Board*)

Plate 5 (below) The interior of St Leonard's Church, formerly the chapel-without-the-walls of Kirkstead Abbey, Lincolnshire. The high quality of the Early English work is evident in the capitals and roof bosses. The wooden screen is one of the earliest in existence (*A. F. Kersting*)

Plate 6 A string of barges used for river maintenance underway at Roswell Pits, Ely. A remnant of the once extensive commercial traffic on Fenland waterways (*K. A. Hitch*)

The smaller sailing boats which had been designed for the waters on which they sailed, were replaced by national and international class racing dinghies which are in many ways unsuitable for use on narrow rivers, often shallow and impeded with weed growth near the banks and with clumps of trees and other obstacles interrupting the flow of the wind. Furthermore, the introduction of guillotine lock gates has made it essential to be able to lower a boat's mast if the owner is not content to confine his sailing to one small stretch of water. A boat adapted to the conditions on Fenland rivers should therefore be reasonably stable, be fitted with a centreboard (or leeboards) and with a tabernacle for lowering the mast, and be heavy enough to carry its way when blanketed by trees and other obstacles. All these requirements were met by the Humber Keel.

Many of the racing clubs have moved away from the river to nearby gravel pits in search of more open and less crowded waters. This has tended to widen still further the division between the racing and cruising fraternities which had already resulted from the virtual, but fortunately not quite complete, disappearance of sailing cruisers from the Fenland rivers.

It is to accommodate the ever-increasing number of motor cruisers that more and more marinas are being built. At the same time, there is pressure and enthusiasm for enlarging the cruising area. The locks between St Ives and Eaton Socon were restored by the Great Ouse Catchment Board as part of a pre-war combined drainage and navigation scheme. Voluntary labour has been a feature of post-war activity, under the aegis of the Great Ouse Restoration Society, and already six further locks have been restored or replaced, so that only one now remains to be reopened in order to re-establish navigation as far upstream as Bedford.

Both the Nene and the Witham are open to pleasure cruisers from the Wash up to Northampton and to Lincoln and the Trent, respectively. Furthermore, it is possible for those who are sufficiently determined and suitably equipped to proceed from the Ouse to the Nene or vice versa by way of the drains of the Middle Level. Primarily, though, the Middle Level is the playground of anglers rather than of those who mess about in boats and strong opposition has been voiced to proposals for making the Middle Level more accessible to pleasure boats.

The overcrowded state of the Norfolk Broads in summer has led to a revival of earlier proposals for a link between the headwaters of the Waveney and the Little Ouse, so that cruisers could travel from the Broads to the Fens and vice versa. Although the two rivers have their sources quite close together, the distance between the heads of the navigable rivers is actually 40 miles in a straight line—and further than that by river—so the problems are formidable.

Angling

Fishing in the Fens has always been famous; the number of eel-rents recorded in the Domesday Book for the area attests to that, but it was not until the late nineteenth century that people had the time or inclination to take up angling as a recreation. Since that time the quality and variety of its coarse fishing has attracted many anglers to the Fens. As long ago as 1900, the London Anglers Association was renting fishing rights on the Ouse, and it is now a common sight to see coachloads of fishermen disembarking on Sunday mornings for a day's sport on the rivers. The larger rivers are popular venues for match fishing and the National Championships have been held in the area several times in recent years.

Pollution of rivers is one of the main problems today, but even in the 1920s, fish were being killed by effluent from the local beet sugar factories, which had only recently been set up. Actions for damages were taken and the effluent disposal system soon improved. Compared to rivers, say, in the Midlands, Fenland waters are relatively free of pollution at the moment, the main causes of concern being industrial effluent and domestic detergents from the towns, and seepage of agricultural chemicals, including silage waste, from the rural areas. In very hot weather some rivers, particularly the Cam below Cambridge, become seriously de-oxygenated, leading to considerable loss of fish. River traffic can be a disturbance to anglers during the holiday season, but the recently constructed Great Ouse Relief Channel and the Cut-off Channel have added several miles of water available to anglers without fear of boat disturbance.

The Fenland is particularly famous for the quality and size of its bream, often reaching 6lb or more, which are common in the Ouse, Nene, Welland and Witham and larger drains. Roach are plentiful, but not of great size; rudd are not quite so common, but of good quality. Tench are sometimes difficult to locate, but fish very well, while many good perch are landed, particularly from the Forty Foot Drain. Dace are plentiful but very subject to pollution. Pike and zander provide excellent sport, with fish quite commonly scaling 20lb. Eels still abound, but are not popular among anglers, except with that dedicated band of night fishing specimen hunters.

Game fish do occur; a salmon was caught in the Huntingdon Ouse in 1967, and the occasional sea trout will run up the same river, but it is usually in the higher reaches of the Cam and the smaller rivers that trout can be found.

Ice Skating

There is a saying in the Fenland that it takes ice to meet old friends, meaning that fenmen gather wherever hard frosts bring ice to the flooded washes and drains. Skating must have begun as a practical necessity in the fens, for in a hard winter, taking to the ice was the only means of communication; there are in existence examples

71

of bone skates and sledge runners that were used to carry people and produce along the frozen rivers before iron-shod skates came into common use during the eighteenth century.

The first competitive skating seems to have evolved from the habits of labourers who, put out of work by the hard weather, would skate from pub to pub along the rivers, with the first arrival being treated to beer by the slower skaters. Opinion varies as to what was the first organised skating match but there are records of a race from Wisbech to Whittlesey in 1763, the winning time for the 15 miles being 46 min. Whittlesey Mere remained a very popular venue for skaters until its drainage in 1851—it was the largest lake in south-east England, and froze smoothly, being very shallow and quick to bear.

The first speed skating competition between individuals involving several turns over a relatively short course seems to have taken place in 1814, when Youngs of Mepal beat Thompson of Wimblington. In 1820 at Crowland, a race of 2 miles was run for a prize of 5 guineas. Already the tradition of local and family champions was becoming established: Young and Gittam of Nordelph, and the Staples brothers from Crowland were the top skaters of those early days, when the rivers were slower running than today and thus more prone to freezing, and when the washes stayed flooded for longer periods during the winter. The skaters were working men, often doing their day's work before taking to the ice to race in competitions in which they might win money or food such as beef or flour. They raced on long fen runners or patterns, evolved from the Dutch introduction of iron-shod skates. Seemingly clumsy, but capable of tremendous speed, especially on the long straight courses typical of the fen drains. The organisation of speed competitions was improved by the founding, in 1827, of the National Skating Association, and almost immediately skaters were drawn in from other parts of the country to compete with the fenmen.

From 1850 to the end of the century, Welney was the home of all the champions: the Smart family, 'Turkey', 'Fish' and James, reigned supreme with the See family from the same village. In 1888 James Smart and 'Gutty' See were first and second in a World Championship race in Holland.

Many private wagers were won and lost on skating matches of all kinds; in 1870 a Fenland champion (possibly Larman Register of Southery, although he must have been well past his prime) raced and beat the Lynn to London train between Littleport and Ely, despite the nobbling of his course by supporters of the railway!

In the early 1890s, the Norwegian type of skate was introduced, which made turning on the ice much easier; these were adopted by all the professional fen skaters, James Smart in particular being responsible for their spread as he held the distribution rights.

1895 was a grand winter for ice; Turkey Smart and Gutty See skated an exhibition match watched by a crowd of 9,000. A E Tebbit of Wentworth became amateur champion and James Smart the professional winner. By this time several of the top skaters had been going to Holland and Switzerland for training. In that winter, probably the greatest race that has ever been held in the Fens was run. The competitors skated from Bottisham Lock to Ely, returned, and set out once more for Ely. After a distance of 30 miles, the result was a dead heat between Tebbit and H A Palmer. Norwegian runners were now used almost exclusively, together with the Norwegian style—long stride, body forward and hands tight behind the back, a much neater way of progression compared to the flailing arms of the old style fenmen.

In 1908 many records were broken by F Dix of Raunds and Greenhall of Landbeach. Dix was sent to the winter Olympic Games, but came nowhere. 1929 was probably the last of the the great seasons to be dominated by fen skaters. Horn of Upwell, Pearson of Mepal and Scott of

Welney shared the honours, and although Horn was still winning in 1931, the names of Londoners from the speedy ice-rink clubs were beginning to appear; the golden era of fen skaters seemed to have ended. Skating still goes on, however, and in spite of a succession of mild winters, the waters of Bury Fen, Swavesey and Whittlesey washes are ready in most seasons for the frosts. The news of bearing ice travels quickly across the fen and sets the locals skating well into the night by the light of their car headlamps.

One by-product of ice skating in the Fens was bandy or hockey on ice which began as early as 1814 when the Bury Fen club was formed. Several villages had teams although it was not until the 1890s that the Bury club had its rules accepted as standard. The club toured Holland in 1890–91, until then unbeaten. The modern game of ice hockey has now taken its place.

5   The Abbeys of the Fens

THE first monasteries and nunneries to be founded in the Fens were places of refuge, places in which God could be worshipped in relative safety and peace in a country torn by constant strife. Of the five monasteries founded in the seventh and eighth centuries, three—Ely (founded 673), Thorney (670) and Crowland (716)—were situated in the heart of the Fenland itself; the others were Peterborough (665), on the edge of the higher ground to the west, and Bardney, near Lincoln (about 700).

All these early monasteries were destroyed and plundered by Danish invaders about the year 870. It was a century later before the monasteries were refounded and then Ramsey (c 969), on another Fenland island, was added to their number. Three other houses were founded before the Normans came: a nunnery at Chatteris (c 980) and priories at Swavesey and Spalding, the latter initially dependent on Crowland but later to achieve independence and considerable wealth.

Thus, at the time of the Domesday survey in 1086, nine out of the sixty monastic houses in England and Wales were in the Fenland. A large proportion perhaps, but hardly significant enough to justify the often-made claim that the Fenland had special attractions to those seeking the monastic life. But these foundations were of the greatest importance to the Fenland because several of them constituted the nuclei around which towns later developed.

With the coming of the Normans, the older houses were refounded and many new ones established. Ely, which had been the second richest monastery in England and Wales at the time of Domesday, was now raised to the status of a cathedral with a Monk Bishop at its head. The Normans were great builders and the fabric of the older monasteries was rebuilt then; the remains of some of their work is still visible today.

Between the Norman conquest and the suppression of the monasteries in the sixteenth century, about another 65 religious houses were founded in the Fenland or its immediate vicinity. Some of these had only a short life, some were very small cells having only one or two monks, while others, such as Kirkstead, Revesby, Anglesey, Barnwell, Pentney, Barlings, Catley, Haverholme and Sempringham, were of moderate size, rivalling in their establishments (but not their wealth) the earlier foundations.

The earlier monasteries and nunneries all followed the rule of St Benedict. Later foundations often followed stricter rules or rules established for particular purposes, and a great variety of kinds of religious house grew up. It may tell us something about the independence of the people of the Fens that the most highly centralised order of all, that of Cluny, was never established there, while the only order to be founded in England during the Middle Ages, the Gilbertines, had its origin in south Lincolnshire. It is curious, however, that the strictest order of all, the Carthusian, which allowed no contact with the outer world at all, did not find its isolation in the wastes of the medieval Fenland, though Swavesey, on the southern fen edge, did for a time follow the rule. Indeed, very few of the Norman and later houses were in the fens themselves. Rather, they were sited on the fen margin or on the silt ridge along the Lincolnshire coast, so that one wonders whether the attraction of the fens arose more from its wealth of wildlife and fish (an important item in the monastic diet) than from its relative isolation in an age when communications were beginning to improve for the first time since the departure of the Romans.

As the monasteries developed, so the range of their functions grew and most of them became, in modern parlance, multi-purpose institutions attempting to provide social services at a time when this was not considered a function of government. Thus they were seats of learning, places of worship, centres of the arts, pioneers of settled agriculture and examples of law and order. The monks and nuns lived an ordered existence, each contributing to the common good, and brought to their daily tasks a dignity which was lacking elsewhere.

The nobles often sent their sons to monasteries as part of their education—Edward the Confessor was a pupil at Ely—and a few had schools at which poor children were taught to read and write as well as to sing in the church. Thorney and Crowland established reputations as centres of literary culture and were famous for their schools of calligraphy and illumination. The noble architecture of the abbey buildings was another manifestation of monastic patronage of the applied arts and this extended right down to details of water supply and drainage, which were far in advance of those in military and domestic buildings of the medieval period.

The monasteries also provided accommodation for travellers, a service which could be a severe drain on the finances since guests did not have to pay for their lodging and entertainment. The arrival of the king, for example, with a large band of retainers, and probably without much notice, no doubt caused consternation and some panic. Some kings were, however, generous to the monasteries at which they stayed, though others were not. Important guests lodged with the abbot or prior, while ordinary travellers were accommodated in the guest house or almonry.

Infirmaries for the sick and elderly monks formed part

of a monastery, though a few monasteries also built hospitals and almhouses outside their gates for lay people, some being specifically for lepers. In addition, there were a number of independent hospitals in use at various periods; these were often in charge of a master or prior belonging to one of the monastic orders. The parish church at Ramsey is generally thought to have been built as the main hall of a large hospital (c 1180). It follows the usual hospital plan with aisles in which the beds would have been placed with their heads to the wall.

Chapels often formed part of hospitals, and similar buildings were sometimes erected outside the gates of a monastery, for the use of women and others who were not permitted within the precincts. Among these are the Norman chapel at Barnwell (Cambridge) which formed part of the Leper Hospital of St Mary Magdalene and two Early English examples: the Church of St Andrew the Less in Cambridge and St Leonard's Chapel, Kirkstead, which were 'chapels-without-the-gate' of Barnwell Priory and Kirkstead Abbey respectively.

St Leonard's is especially enchanting and displays workmanship of very high quality in the stiff-leaf capitals of the shafts of windows, west doorway and vaulting, and in the roof bosses, as shown in Pl 4, p 67. The thirteenth-century wooden screen and the marble effigy of a knight are among the very earliest of their kind; the door, too, and the ironwork on it are as old as the chapel itself.

In spite of having been used as a store for many years, the Barnwell leper chapel survives as a simple Norman building with elaborately decorated chancel arch and doorways, and several original windows. Two thirteenth-century buildings which were formerly the chapels of the Hospitals of St John and St Mary Magdalene, united about 1240, are in West End, Ely, the smaller one having a carved stone above the doorway which may be several centuries older.

Kirkstead Abbey seems to have been something of an industrial centre in the twelfth century, as it is recorded that it had 'four forges, two for smelting and two for working iron, with the right to dig for ore and to take dead wood for fuel'. Alas, no visible evidence remains of this early industry!

The abbot or prior of a wealthy monastery was a powerful local personality, responsible for the maintenance of law and order on the monastic demesne and often outside it. In the case of Ely in the thirteenth century, the demesnes of the cathedral and the convent included the whole of the Isle of Ely, substantial areas in east Suffolk and central Norfolk and a great many manors in neighbouring counties. Consequently the monasteries played a major part in local affairs, appointing mayors, holding fairs and helping to build and maintain roads and bridges. In the Fens, bridges were essential to provide access for pilgrims and other travellers and the tolls payable for their use were a source of revenue to the monastery that built them. Crowland and Spalding are among the monasteries whose bridge building activities are recorded.

Besides the monks and nuns, there were also the friars. Several orders of friars established themselves in England early in the thirteenth century, building convents in the principal towns from which to carry out their preaching and missionary work—not so much the conversion of those who had not been baptised in the Church, as the combating of heresy. The buildings of a friary were simple and might comprise a few town houses and a garden; they did not necessarily need to be special purpose buildings of the kind established by the monks, often in remote parts of the country. The four main orders established houses in Boston, King's Lynn and Cambridge, those in Cambridge being mainly for students of their respective order and later being absorbed into the present colleges of the university. At King's Lynn, the tall octagonal tower of the Greyfriars

church stands in a public garden in St James's Street—
an elegant and moving monument to an important
medieval institution which has left few material remains.
The much less impressive Whitefriars gateway also
exists at the southern end of the town.

At the Reformation, all these religious houses were
suppressed and largely destroyed. The stone from which
they were built was a precious commodity in the
Fenland, and much of it has been re-used by Cambridge
colleges or in nearby domestic buildings.

The two largest and finest churches of all, Ely and
Peterborough, were re-established as secular cathed-
rals. Other monastic churches, or parts of them, at
Bourne, Crowland, Deeping St James, Freiston, South
Kyme and Thorney, have continued in use as parish
churches, and as we have already noted, the hospital of
Ramsey abbey is the present parish church of the town.

Ely Cathedral

From whichever direction the visitor approaches Ely,
the silhouette of the cathedral stands out on the skyline,
with its single tower at the west end and, over the
crossing, the wide and comparatively squat octagon
crowned by an octagonal lantern (Pl 11, p 87). Turrets
and pinnacles abound. It is a silhouette without parallel
among British churches.

Of the nunnery built in the seventh century by
Etheldreda, Queen of Northumbria, and of the Saxon
monastery which Hereward the Wake used as his
headquarters in resisting the Normans, nothing remains
today. The present buildings were begun by Simeon, the
first Norman abbot, in 1083 and to them the shrine of St
Etheldreda was translated in 1106. Three years later,
Ely was made the see of a bishop. The prior then
became head of the monastery and the abbot established
his bishop's palace to the west of the monastery.

The visitor does well to approach the cathedral from
this end, across Palace Green. The symmetry and

stylistic coherence of the Norman west front are broken today of the absence of a transept on the north side of the central tower and by the superposition of the Early English porch (or Galilee). The decoration is provided by rows of blank arcading, each row being different from the others. The octagonal motif is already here, in the corners of the tower, though the octagonal upper storey was added after the rebuilding of the crossing (the transept turrets actually have ten faces—twelfth-century decimalisation, perhaps?).

After passing through the Galilee, with its unusual tracery, wall arcading in two layers and vaulted roof, the visitor arrives under the Norman west tower. To the right is the west transept, built several years later than the nave and displaying the decorative motifs characteristic of late Norman architecture: zig-zag work around the openings and intersecting arches in the blank arcading on the walls.

On entering the nave, the immediate impression is one of great length and height but comparative narrowness; this effect is increased by the shafts on the inside of each column which carry the eye straight up to the wooden roof. The twelve bays of the nave are as the Normans built them, giving a feeling of solidity and rythmic uniformity at each vertical stage, broken only slightly by the alternation in the design of the piers.

Then at the crossing, one is suddenly on the open, in a space three bays across in each direction and with light flooding through the lantern overhead, from the ends of the transepts, the choir and the nave, and also diagonally from the large fourteenth-century windows of the noble octagon. This octagon was the conception of Alan of Walsingham, who held office as sacrist in 1322 when the Norman tower over the crossing collapsed. Though the lantern appears to be supported on a comparatively delicate wooden vault springing from the eight corners of the octagon, this is actually an illusion: the weight is taken by an ingenious system of hidden beams (the largest parts of which are 3ft 4in by 2ft 2in in cross-section) arranged on the hammerbeam principle. A model in the south transept illustrates this supreme example of medieval carpentry, the work, we can be almost sure, of William Hurle, Chief Carpenter to the King's works south of the Trent from 1336 to 1354. Stone heads of sacrist, carpenter, abbot and prior responsible for the rebuilding are on the arches surrounding the octagon.

The transepts are the oldest parts of the building. In them the pattern of the piers, gallery and clerestory is generally similar to that of the nave, but is simpler in style. There are aisles on either side of the transepts, those to the east being used as chapels. At the ends, later windows have been inserted and a narrow balcony constructed at gallery level. Both transepts have hammerbeam roofs with angels as supporters of the hammerbeam. These roofs date from the fifteenth century and today both roofs and angels are gaily coloured.

The original choir, now reduced to three bays by the building of the octagon, stopped short at the Norman piers by the east end of the choir stalls and was completed by an apsidal chancel, as in almost all Norman churches. It soon proved too small; the apse was pulled down and replaced by a much larger retrochoir of six bays in the Early English style, with a decorative vaulted roof springing from Purbeck marble capitals and with lancet windows in two rows at the east end. This was the work of Bishop Hugh of Northwold and was built between 1234 and 1252.

The first three bays of the choir were rebuilt at the time the octagon was constructed, in the style of fourteenth-century gothic with much ornamentation on the tracery, the surrounding arches and the sills of the openings. The vault above is a lierne vault, with mouldings running in all directions and bosses wherever they meet.

The Lady Chapel is a freestanding building, now joined to the cathedral only at the north-east corner of the north transept, though originally entered through the ornate doorway in the chancel aisle. It was begun just before the collapse of the central tower, but further work was postponed until 1335–53. The visitor entering from the cathedral is at once struck by its brightness, the medieval stained glass having been replaced with clear glass in the flowing Decorated windows on every side. Beneath the windows are seats supporting three-dimensional ogee arches, heavily ornamented with figures, which give what Pevsner describes as a 'vivid impression of a movement swinging and rocking forward and upward'. Wider niches at intervals are twice repeated on the walls between the windows and carry the eye up to the finely-detailed lierne vault above.

The two chantry chapels at the east end of the cathedral are even more ornate and the veritable forest of spikes in Bishop Alcock's has to be seen to be believed. Bishop West's chantry is more restful and has a roof which combines classical ornament with Gothic design; it also has a particularly fine pair of sixteenth-century iron gates.

The monuments at Ely are of all periods from the seventh century onwards. Those of special interest include the simple shaft and base of Ovin's cross in the south aisle of the nave (Ovin was the steward of St Etheldreda), and the monuments to Bishops Nigellus (1169), Kilkenny (1257) and Northwold (a particularly sumptuous one of 1254). Between them, they form a gallery illustrating the development of sculpture since the twelfth century.

Finally, there are the very fine fourteenth-century choir stalls, sixty of them retaining the original misericords under the seats depicting real and fanciful scenes from medieval life.

THE ABBEYS OF THE FENS
Ely—The Precinct

Of the other buildings of the monastery, a fair number remain, though they have been much altered in the course of time. Some house parts of The King's School and others are private dwellings. They form a pleasant group which should not be missed.

A few bays of the cloister survive in the angle between the south transept and the south aisle of the nave. Between the aisle and the cloister is the Monk's Door, an elaborately carved trefoiled archway dating from the mid-twelfth century, with figures of monsters and monks. Further to the west, and accessible only from the cathedral, is the even more elaborate Prior's Door: a superb tour-de-force of medieval carving. The tympanum carries a seated figure of Christ supported by two angels and all around, on the arches and piers, are deeply carved foliage scrolls augmented by human and animal figures.

On the south side of the cloister, the Bishop's House has been built into the Great Hall of the monastery and beyond it, but separated from it by the site of the former Prior's Kitchen, is the Prior's House, built round a Norman vaulted undercroft with a fourteenth-century hall above it.

Attached to the Prior's House is Prior Crauden's Chapel. It is quite tiny, though comparatively tall. The decoration is as rich as that in the Lady Chapel and it was built at the same period. The mosaic pavement of geometrical, animal and vegetable motifs comprises irregular tiles painted in different colours; Adam and Eve and the serpent are represented on the floor in the front of the altar.

The Headmaster's House (of the King's School) is built into the fourteenth-century Queen's Hall of the monastery and on its west side adjoins a long building, now known as the storehouse, which runs towards Ely Porta—the great gatehouse of the monastery. The

Plate 7 (above) Denver Sluice from the air. The widened Denver Sluice is on the left and the head sluice to the Relief Channel in the centre, with the impounding sluice across the Cut-off Channel below it. The diversion sluice for the Ely Ouse-Essex water transfer scheme and the residual flow sluice were still under construction when this photograph was taken (*Cambridge University Committee for Aerial Photography*)

Plate 8 (below) Tulip fields near Spalding in Lincolnshire (*A. F. Kersting*)

Plate 10 (*above*) Anglesey Abbey. The photograph shows three of the intimate formal gardens near the house which form part of a larger scheme in which grass, trees and statuary predominate (*The National Trust*)

Plate 9 (*opposite*) Wind pump on Wicken Fen in Cambridgeshire (*A. F. Kersting*)

Plate 11 (*below*) The great octagon and the west tower at Ely, seen across the park from the site of the former Norman castle (*K. A. Hitch*)

Plate 12 (*above*) Mute swans on flooded washland at Sutton Gault, with the embankment of the Bedford river in the background (*K. Sellers*)

Plate 13 (*below*) Evening on Wicken Fen, Cambridgeshire (*A. F. Kersting*)

THE ABBEYS OF THE FENS

building of this was begun in 1397 and its square corner
turrets contrast with the wealth of polygonal work on
the cathedral.

The Infirmary lay to the south-east of the south
transept of the cathedral. Originally a late Norman
aisled hall, with a chapel at the east end, it was
reconstructed in the fourteenth century: the nave then
became a roofless lane and the aisles were made into
separate houses on the fronts of which the arcading
may still be seen. One of these houses was built by Alan
of Walsingham for his own use. The arch at the end of
the lane separated the hall of the infirmary from the
chapel, part of which is now incorporated in the
Deanery.

The range of buildings on the north side of the
precinct has been very much restored. It includes two
gates—the timber-framed Steeple Gate and the stone
Sacristy Gate—with the Goldsmith's Tower between
them and the former Almonry to their east.

To the west of the cathedral is the Bishop's Palace. Its
oldest parts are the eastern red-brick tower and the
lower sections of the western tower, both the work of
Bishop Alcock (1486-1501). The western tower was
completed and the wing added to it in 1550. The rest of
the present building, which joins the two towers, is
seventeenth-century work, extended and remodelled
inside in 1771. It is now used as a school for handi-
capped children.

Peterborough Cathedral and Precinct

The Benedictine Abbey of Peterborough was founded by
Peada, King of Mercia, in 655. Like other Fenland
monasteries it was sacked by the Danes in 870 and
rebuilt about a hundred years later. This (second) Saxon
monastery was in turn sacked by Hereward the Wake
and later destroyed in a fire in 1116; there are remains
of the church below the south transept and some stones
from it are displayed in the cathedral.

The present cathedral was begun in 1118. Because it is closely surrounded by other buildings in the precinct and by the buildings of the city, it is not easily seen as a whole and it nowhere dominates the skyline as Ely does. Rather, one comes upon it by surprise on entering the close.

Most visitors approach the cathedral from the Market Place through the Outer Gate of the monastery and are immediately brought face to face with the giant niches of the west front. These were added in the thirteenth century and are the result of one of several changes of plan in treating the west end. Opinions about them differ, but it is hard not to recognise that their proportions do not relate to those on the wall behind, which forms part of a previous scheme, and that the whole appearance would be considerably improved by the removal of the Perpendicular central porch, fine as it is in itself.

Inside, we see the Norman church, almost in its entirety. The nave is generally similar to that at Ely, but the details of the piers and arches are less ponderous and more ornate, a reflection of the fact that not only was the building at Peterborough commenced later but also that it proceeded more slowly. The progression from the chancel to the crossing and westwards along the nave occupied a period of about 70 years and is marked by changes in the details of the architecture, which do not always correspond on the two sides of the church.

The chancel is thus the oldest part of the cathedral. It retains its apse, though the smaller apses at the ends of the aisles were swept away when the elegant fan-vaulted retrochoir—the newest part of the church—was added by Abbot Kirton about 1500. The very close affinity between the vaults at Peterborough and those in King's College Chapel, Cambridge, has led to a suggestion that both were designed by John Wastell.

The aisles of the chancel, nave and transepts are

vaulted and their walls decorated with blank intersecting arcading. From the south aisle, two doors lead
into the cloister; the eastern, or Canon's Door, is
Norman work at its best and is finely ornamented with
carved foliage and zig-zag work.

The squat tower over the crossing is a rebuilt version
of one that was erected to replace a higher Norman one
which was taken down after the tower at Ely collapsed
—doubtless in order to avoid a similar disaster. At one
time, it was crowned with a wooden octagonal lantern.

The ceilings of the nave and transepts are the original
ones. They date from about 1220 and are painted with
bold lozenge patterns enclosing figures of saints, arch-
bishops, kings, queens and also monsters; they constitute
one of the outstanding features of the cathedral. The
partly-vaulted and highly ornamented chancel ceiling is
also wooden—it was erected in the fifteenth century.

Four separate plans for treating the west end can be
identified. In the first, towers were to be erected over
the ninth aisle bays (counting from the crossing). It was
then decided to lengthen the nave and to add transepts
crowned by small towers—the north one of these was
built but is barely visible from inside the precinct. The
third plan was to build seven bays of niches outside the
west wall as a part of a screen extending the whole
width of the transepts. This plan was then modified to
give a much larger niche on either side of the central
one and the square turrets outside them. The porch was
added later.

Among the various monuments to abbots and bishops
at the east end, there is an extremely important piece of
Anglo-Saxon sculpture, known as the Hedda Stone or
Monk's Stone, dating from about 800 and depicting the
twelve apostles.

Of the rest of the monastery, rather less survives than
at Ely. It comprises two walls of the cloister, of which
that on the lavatorium side is richly panelled; the
remains of the infirmary; two undercrofts in the former

abbot's lodging (now the Bishop's Palace); and a number of buildings outside the west end of the cathedral.

The infirmary has been treated as at Ely, the nave having been opened up to form a lane with houses built into the arcading and at the end of the chapel.

Near the west end of the cathedral are three gates: the Norman Outer Gate leading to the Market Place, the thirteenth-century gate leading to what is now the Bishop's Palace and the richly decorated sixteenth-century Priory Gate on the north side of the precinct. The King's Lodging and Abbot's Prison which adjoin the Outer Gate are also largely medieval.

Other Monastic Remains

The parish church at Bourne retains the proportions of the original abbey church and the arcading of the four-bay Norman nave. The canons (it was an Augustinian house) started to rebuild the west end about 1200 and what remains is the result of piecemeal development of a two-tower front, of which only one tower was ever completed—and that not for another two hundred years.

At Deeping St James we have the whole priory church: nave, chancel and south aisle, since there never was a north aisle and plans for the building of a central tower seem to have been abandoned quite early on. There are some unusual and very fine architectural features in the church: the seven-bay late twelfth-century arcade and the thirteen pointed triforium arches above it, with a passage behind them having only four tiny external windows; the double piscina, the seven blank arches on corbels next to it and the heavily-moulded circular window arches in the south side of the nave; and the very fine Norman font of Caen stone. The tower was added early in the eighteenth century and combines 'medieval' features in a design that is classical in feeling.

It is likely that at Deeping the monks used the nave and allowed the parishioners and guilds to worship in the aisle. The situation at Croyland (Crowland) must have been similar as the preserved north aisle is of similar proportions to the ruined monastic nave and much wider than the south aisle.

Croyland Abbey was founded in 716 on the island site of St Guthlac's cell, traces of the floor of which have been uncovered outside the west end of the south aisle. This first abbey was pillaged and destroyed by the Danes about 860 and was rebuilt about a hundred years later. This Saxon abbey was in turn destroyed by a disastrous fire in 1091, and the next rebuilding was disrupted by an earthquake in 1117 and a fire in 1146. But the monks persevered.

Apart from the parish church in the north aisle, the west front of the nave is almost complete and there are some piers and arches beyond it. Nothing of the crossing, transepts or east end remains. It is the west front of the nave that attracts attention with its niches and figures and the quatrefoil over the door illustrating incidents in the life of St Guthlac. The present church retains its vaulted roof, a comparatively rare feature in the Fenland; its solid but squat west tower was added in the fifteenth century.

Of the nearby rival abbey of Thorney, the nave has been retained as the parish church, the Norman arcades and gallery openings having been blocked in when the church was restored in 1638 following the draining of the surrounding fens. Again it is the west front which impresses, tall and dignified with its Norman angle turrets, Perpendicular battlements and partly blocked Perpendicular window.

St Margaret's church, King's Lynn, seems to have served both as the parish church of the 'new town' of Lynn from its foundation about 1100 and as the church of the adjacent priory, of which a range of buildings survives. Otherwise, how can one explain the ambitious plan of the Norman church, with its two ornate western towers, begun some fifty years before the town was important enough to receive a charter from King John?

The present church is a mixture of styles, with its Early English chancel and transepts, Perpendicular clerestory and a nave rebuilt in 1741 after the collapse of the spire over the crossing. Among the furnishings are some fine fourteenth-century screens, an early Georgian pulpit with superb marquetry work on the tester and panelling, two of the largest and finest brasses in England (Adam de Walsokne †1349 and Robert Braunche †1364, with their wives) and some excellent modern letter cutting by John Skelton, a pupil of Eric Gill.

Of both Freiston and South Kyme priories, parts of the nave and one aisle survive in the present churches. Freiston has a nave of no less than nine bays of which six are Norman and have fascinating hood-moulds ending in long-snouted monsters. South Kyme is much smaller and is now disused, but its finest feature, the ambitious Norman south doorway, may be seen without entering.

Parts of the monastic buildings have been incorporated into domestic buildings at Anglesey Abbey (see p 158), Ramsey Abbey, Swaffham Bulbeck Priory and Winnold Priory. Much more substantial remains exist of the Benedictine nunnery of St Radegund in Cambridge, which was suppressed in 1497 and replaced by Jesus College.

The original monastic church is now the college chapel, though considerably reduced in size. The style is mostly Early English, as are the three arches which formed the west front of the chapter house, still visible in the cloister outside. The visitor should look for the fine transept ceilings, the fascinating carved bench ends and the nineteenth-century stained glass by Morris and Co, to designs by Burne-Jones, William Morris and Ford Madox Brown. Other parts of the monastic buildings are incorporated in the Master's Lodge to the west of the chapel.

At Isleham, there remains an unaltered but very small early Norman church. This can only have been the church of the priory established there for two or three monks about the year 1200. The nave, chancel and apsidal east end are all there, though the latter has lost its vault. There are several small Norman windows as well as two later ones, and a fine chancel arch. After many years use as a barn, the building is now in the care of the Department of the Environment; a notice on the door directs visitors to the custodian of the key.

Denny Priory (TL 492686), north of Waterbeach, is also in the care of the Department of the Environment, whose workmen are excavating and restoring it. It was occupied in succession by monks from Ely, by the Knights Templars, by the Knights Hospitallers and, finally, by Franciscan nuns of the Order of St Clare, who were formerly at Waterbeach. It constitutes the only extensive remains in Britain of a house of the poor Clares, as they are known.

The nuns replaced the chancel and apse of the original Norman church with a large square, aisled church and converted the Norman nave into rooms, some of which formed the abbess's lodging; to this the present farmhouse is attached. The nun's church to the east of the original crossing has disappeared. They built their domestic buildings to the east of the monk's cloister and, of these, the refectory survives along the south side of the court.

At Ramsey, part of the gatehouse survives and is owned by the National Trust. It was built about 1500 and is unusually ornate, with panelled buttresses and friezes around the doorway and the oriel window above. Inside is the marble tomb of Ailwin (Eolwin) who founded the abbey in the tenth century; the tomb, however, is later and dates from about 1230. Another part of this same gatehouse is at Hinchingbrooke, near

Huntingdon, whence it was transported after the dissolution of the monastery.

An imposing flint gatehouse is all that remains of Pentney Priory (TF 702122), an Augustinian house founded before 1135 by the river Nar. South of the river, in the village of Marham, are the foundations and south wall of the nave of a Cistertian nunnery, containing two large circular windows, and part of the west range of the cloister.

Of the other monastic buildings in the Fenland and on the fen margin, hardly anything remains above ground for the visitor to see. Some, like Bardney, Sawtry and Sempringham, have been excavated so that we know what they were like. Sempringham is a particularly sad loss, as it was the Mother Church of the Gilbertine Order, in which canons and nuns lived in separate cloisters and worshipped in a church divided longitudinally by a solid wall. Of the wealthy priory of Spalding, around which the present town grew, one finds only hints in names such as the Prior's Oven and Abbey Buildings, but their provenance is uncertain.

Three miles north-east of Spalding, however, is the elegant Wykeham Chapel, built by Prior Hatfield in 1311 as the private chapel of his country house. Although less ornate and roofless, it is similar in quality, size and height to Prior Crauden's Chapel at Ely. An unusual feature is the roof line of a former building—perhaps a priest's house—cutting into the west window of the chapel.

Hereward the Wake

No account of the Fenland abbeys would be complete without reference to Hereward the Wake, the rebellious leader of a band of Anglo-Saxon fugitives whose true story has been complicated by legend and conjecture. He was a Lincolnshire man, possibly the son of Leofric, Earl of Mercia, though it is more likely that early historians exaggerated his family connections and that his father was a certain Leofric of Bourne. In his early years he travelled in Britain and on the continent, and in 1070, hearing that Cnut's heir, the Danish King Sweyn, was about to attack England in an effort to recover his uncle's kingdom, he joined a party of Danish invaders and sacked Peterborough Abbey, killing many and making off with much treasure. He later claimed that he was just trying to prevent the church valuables from falling into Norman hands. Sweyn then unexpectedly made peace with William and Hereward retreated to a refuge on the Isle of Ely, where he was joined by Morcar, Earl of Northumbria.

There is no doubt that William took the rebellion seriously for he marched north and laid siege to the Isle. Legend tells how Hereward gained entry to the king's camp at Brandon, disguised on his mare Swallow, and learnt the plan of attack on the Isle. Hereward is said to have killed a knight in the camp, before escaping to the fens.

Later, again disguised, he joined a pressed party of local labourers who were building a causeway to Aldreth from the south and at an opportune moment fired the reeds, once more thwarting his enemy.

Eventually it appears that the monks at Ely became tired of the siege and revealed the way across the fen to William; nevertheless the abbey had to pay a heavy fine. Hereward apparently made his escape, though it is uncertain whether he was granted a pardon by the king or died in an ambush a few years later.

It is strange that such a famous story in English history and literature seems to have generated so little local oral tradition in an area where such tradition is still strong; not one person in the Fens to whom we have spoken, nor any book of Fenland stories we have seen, mentions the name Hereward.

6   Parish Churches and Chapels

Medieval Churches

BEFORE the Norman conquest in 1066, the Fenland was a poor and sparsely populated region. The compilers of the Domesday book recorded no boroughs and the average population of most of the area has been estimated to have been fewer than two-and-a-half persons a square mile.

Within 300 years all this had changed: the population had increased twentyfold and the area contained the greatest concentration of wealth in the whole of rural England. In 1334, when the moveable wealth of the country was assessed for taxation purposes, nearly one-third of all places having an assessed wealth of £225 or over were in the Fenland and Boston was the fifth richest town in England. This phenomenal growth was the result of the expansion of those parishes, mainly on the silt ridge to the south and west of the Wash, which were able to reclaim land from the sea and fens and bring it into production, particularly for sheep rearing.

It was natural that in an age of almost universal faith part of this wealth should be devoted to the building and renewal of parish churches and to their extension to meet the needs of the expanding population. The medieval church was not only used as a place of worship, but was also the centre of the social life of the village. Miracle plays would be performed in it during

Holy Week and at Christmas, beanfeasts took place in the nave at harvest and other times and on the patronal feast day a fair was often held in the churchyard. Villages were proud of their churches and neighbouring parishes vied with each other in their design and decoration, though those which belonged to abbeys, such as Whaplode, Heckington and Over, had an unfair advantage in the matter of resources.

The periods of church building can be identified by the architectural styles and match closely the growth in the wealth of the Fenland villages. Hardly any Saxon work survives, its primitive forms having been swept away by later rebuildings, so that we are left with only the towers at Great Hale, Thurlby and Cambridge (St Bene'ts), and traces elsewhere.

Much Norman work, on the other hand, was sufficiently ambitious to survive subsequent reconstruction and the existence of substantial Norman arcades at Long Sutton, Walsoken, Tilney All Saints, Whaplode and Ely (St Mary) is evidence of sufficient wealth and population to justify large aisled churches as early as the twelfth century. Mostly it is late Norman or Transitional work, in which pointed arches began to replace circular ones but without that lightness and sense of balance that characterise Gothic architecture.

It was, however, during the thirteenth and fourteenth centuries that the wealth of the Fenland reached its peak and it is therefore in the various manifestations of the Gothic style that the finest examples of medieval church architecture are expressed. West Walton, Moulton and Weston stand out among those in the Early English (thirteenth century) style in Fenland parish churches. There are also several fine Early English towers, including those at Leverington, Walsoken, Wainfleet St Mary, Whaplode, Elm, Warboys, Long Sutton (which is unusual in retaining its original lead spire) and Frampton, which has one of the earliest broach spires in England.

Decorated (fourteenth-century) work in the Fenland is among the finest in England; one need think only of the predominately Decorated churches at Heckington, Helpringham, Holbeach, Gedney, Boston, Over and Sutton-in-the-Isle to establish that. There are also very many individual windows and features of comparable quality in other towns and villages.

Church building continued into the fifteenth century throughout the whole of the Fenland, notwithstanding a decline in population and the dramatic effect of the Black Death, 1348–50. Some of the churches in the Perpendicular style were very large so clearly there was still much wealth available. Cambridge (Great St Mary's), Burwell, Terrington St Clement, Walpole St Peter, King's Lynn (St Nicholas), Friskney, Gosberton, Tattershall and Conington are among those which sought to achieve that ideal of light and tranquil spaciousness which was the aim of the later medieval builders.

Strictly speaking, King's Lynn (St Nicholas) is a chapel rather than a church, since it is a chapel of ease to St Margaret's, and it is indeed one of the largest chapels in Britain. Not far away is the very different Red Mount Chapel, a pilgrim's chapel on the way to Walsingham built in 1485. Its exterior is octagonal and above the oblong basement is a cruciform core with a central fan vault reached by staircases between the core and the octagon.

We know very little about the men who designed and built the medieval churches. Much of the carpentry and sculpture was shop work and this doubtless accounts for a number of local peculiarities. Masons, on the other hand, could only do their work on the actual building sites and so travelled from one job to another; it has been possible to trace the movement of some masons by their individual marks. In this way, fashions spread quite rapidly from the larger towns to the more remote villages.

The churches mentioned above are scattered all over the Fenland: along the western fen edge, on the silt ridge around the Wash, in the Norfolk marshland and on the Isle of Ely. A survey of a different kind, for example one based on the quality of their woodwork and roofs rather than on dates, would also have included many churches along the eastern fen edge. There is so much that is worth seeing that any attempt to describe Fenland churches in detail in a single chapter is bound to be unsatisfactory. We can only hope that what is written here is enough to whet readers' appetites, so that they are inspired to go to see for themselves—armed, it goes without saying, with the appropriate volumes in the *Buildings of England* series.

Medieval Church Architecture

There is, of course, no such thing as a typical Fenland church; every one differs from its neighbour and all have features to interest the serious visitor. Some characteristics do, however, occur time and again in Fenland churches: towers are tall and are frequently crowned with spires, porches are wide with gabled roofs, chancels seem to have been restored more heavily in the nineteenth century than other parts of the church and had perhaps been less well maintained in the past, chapels at the sides of the chancels are unusual, and clerestories are well-defined (often an earlier and steeper pre-clerestory roof line is visible inside the church). Polygonal motifs are strong throughout the region, perhaps inspired by the wealth of such work at Ely and Lincoln.

Whatever the quality of stonework or the furnishings, it is the right relationship between the various parts that makes a church look right. Sometimes ambitious plans were not completed, as for example, at Bicker where the bays of the nave seem too grand for so short a church or at Northborough where the rebuilding of the south transept on an ambitious scale has had the effect of dwarfing the rest of the building. Even at Heckington, a church wholly in one style and built at the same time, there is a sense of unease about the relationship between the transepts and the nave, when viewed from the outside.

Needless to say, there are very many other churches which do look just right and where the parts do relate harmoniously to one another. This is easiest to achieve in a building without structural divisions such as King's Lynn (St Nicholas), and becomes progressively more difficult as chancel, transepts and chapels are added. Bottisham, Walpole St Peter and Helpringham are other Fenland churches which score high marks for good proportions. Again, one cannot fail to be impressed by the harmony and nobility of the façade of Swavesey church seen as it is approached from the road.

The high standard of medieval church building also owed much to the ready availability of good quality building stone from the quarries at Barnack, Weldon, Clipsham, Ketton and Ancaster, and the comparative ease with which it could be transported by water to almost any site in the Fenland. Not only are these limestones extracted in large blocks, but their fine grain and homogeneous structure make it possible to cut them in any direction and to carve them readily (hence the name freestone).

A large number of Fenland churches are faced with ashlar—squared masonry blocks laid in horizontal courses like brickwork—rather than with rubble or unhewn stone straight from the quarry. Where the parishioners could not afford to face the whole church with ashlar, it might be used for a part of the building only, often the tower.

Ashlar masonry which is well hewn and well laid is itself a pleasure to behold, even without any ornamentation (see, for example, the nave and aisles at Swaton). Some builders did not stop there, but added friezes and ornamental string courses, inserted niches in the buttresses and gave them ornate pediments, and softened the skyline with openwork or battlemented parapets, bearing pinnacles and spirelets. So we get such tours-de-force as Heckington and Boston.

The carving of gargoyles gave the masons scope for indulging their sense of humour and many took advantage of it. There is a particularly interesting set at Over and the elephant on the tower at Gosberton is well known.

In the southern Fens, freestone was supplemented by clunch, a form of hard chalk that was quarried at Burwell and Reach until quite recently, by brown carstone from quarries near Ely, and by Norfolk flint. Clunch is both easier to carve and less weather-resistant than the oolitic limestones, so is more suitable for interior use.

Brick came into its own for church building towards the end of the medieval period and the Perpendicular parts of Cowbit, Lutton, Wiggenhall St Mary and Wiggenhall St Mary Magdalen are built of it. Later it was insensitively used to repair decayed stonework in a number of churches.

Towers and Spires

Towers and spires are prominent features of almost all medieval Fenland churches. Few are all of one period, most having been heightened by later generations, yet not always finished as intended (for instance, spires were begun but never completed at Gedney and Morton).

Boston Stump, the tallest parochial steeple in Britain, is in a class of its own. It was begun about 1450 and originally designed to comprise two stages and a spire. Instead a belfry stage, unworthy of the highly orna-mented stages below, was added and then a fine stone octagonal lantern with pinnacles and flying buttresses. The interior of the tower is equally remarkable since it is open right up to the vault at the top of the second stage (137ft) and is flooded with light from all sides, in

complete contrast to the gloomy interiors of many
towers at the western end of churches.

Some other Fenland church towers are crowned with
octagons, Sutton-in-the-Isle being one of the best known.
It is richly decorated, with excellent quatrefoil friezes
and battlements, and has two octagonal stages, in the
fashion of Ely. Architectural historians, however, tend
to get more excited about the octagonal upper stage at
Swaffham Prior (St Mary) since this is Norman work
and is earlier than the Ely octagon—its example may
therefore have inspired Alan of Walsingham. Above it
are two 16-sided stages and the whole is now crowned
with a small fibre-glass spire which was placed there by
helicopter. Other octagons are at Upwell, West Dereham
(where one crowns a circular tower) and Methwold,
where a panelled octagon forms the base of a spire.

Polygonal forms also occur lower down the tower,
particularly in Early English work where polygonal
clasping buttresses are often accompanied by blank
arcades with roll mouldings. The finest examples are a
group of churches near Wisbech: Elm, Leverington,
Walsoken, West Walton and Long Sutton. The polygonal
motif continued into the fifteenth century and appears
on the Perpendicular towers at Conington and Peterborough (St John the Baptist).

There is also high quality Early English blank arcading
on the towers at Gedney, Whaplode, Wainfleet St Mary
and King's Lynn (St Nicholas). Gedney is regarded as
the finest of all these towers: the lower part is Early
English with complex clasping buttresses and it is
topped by an ornate Perpendicular bell stage.

Among later towers, that at Heckington combines high
quality masonry and fine proportions with discrete
ornament, while Moulton and Northwold are particularly
fine examples of Perpendicular work.

Spires to the east of the Fens are rare (Methwold and
Wilton are the exceptions) and there are few in the
Norfolk marshland. As soon as one crosses the Nene

Plate 14 Fishing boats at King's Lynn, with the Customs House behind (*East Anglia Tourist Board*)

Plate 15 (*above*) Eighteenth- and nineteenth-century houses in the spacious mainstreet of Upwell reflecting in the old course of the river Nene (*D. Beard*)

Plate 16 (*below*) Nelson Street, King's Lynn. The building in the foreground with brick nogging in the upper storey is part of Hampton Court, an almost complete group of a medieval merchant's buildings, comprising shops, house, office and warehouse (*Lynn News and Advertiser*)

estuary, however, they become quite common and the same is true in the south-western part of the Fens. And what superb spires most of them are!

The lead-covered thirteenth-century spire at Long Sutton has already been mentioned; it is one of the best preserved of its date in England and is accompanied by four small matching spires capping the octagonal corner buttresses.

While there is a good deal of variation in the design of stone spires, most Fenland examples are recessed (that is set back from the edge of the tower) behind battle-ments with corner pinnacles which are sometimes connected to the spire by ornate flying buttresses, usually too delicate to serve any structural purpose. The interiors are lit by dormer windows or lucarnes, commonly in three tiers (Holbeach has four, Yaxley, Quadring and Swineshead only two); these and the angles of the spire provide scope for ornamentation. The spires at Warboys and Frampton are broach spires and others (Heckington, Holbeach and Willingham) combine the two forms in various ways.

It is hard to select the best examples, but it would be difficult not to include Whittlesey (St Mary), Gosberton, Moulton, Over, Leverington, Heckington, Warboys, Helpringham, Spalding, Donington and Billingborough in our list.

No less than ten Fenland churches were originally built with detached towers, an arrangement rare in England. Those at Tydd St Giles, West Walton, Long Sutton and Terrington St John were originally open at the lowest stage and may well have been built in that way in order to offer the minimum resistance to swirling flood waters. All four are very close to the Nene estuary and we know that the predecessor to the present church at Walpole St Peter was swept away in a flood. The tower at Terrington St John was later joined to the church by a two-storey brick building which may have been a chantry house. Fleet logically ought to be included in this group, but its ground floor seems always to have been enclosed.

The towers at Wisbech, Whaplode and Spalding were built later than the churches of which they now form part, while that at Terrington St Clement seems to be the result of a change of plan leading to a decision not to build a tower over the crossing. Donington is the tenth member of the group.

Porches

Although porches have a number of utilitarian functions —some religious and some secular—they also provide great scope for ornamentation. Even in such grand Fenland churches as Walpole St Peter, Heckington, Over and Leverington, the main porch is one of the most ornate parts. Exterior decoration might comprise a sculptured gable, of which that at Heckington, dominated by a seated figure of Christ, is an outstanding example, buttresses with niches—now alas, usually devoid of figures—pinnacles, friezes and battlements.

Inside, the porch might well be the only part of the church to carry a vault, apart from the tower. So we find ornate tierceron vaults at Sutton-in-the-Isle, Upwell and Long Sutton, a lierne-star vault at King's Lynn (St Nicholas) and fan vaults at Burwell and Spalding, some with attractive and amusing carved bosses. The walls provided an opportunity for blank arcading: at Weston and West Walton it is Early English work, at Swineshead, Decorated, and at Soham, Isleham and Terrington St Clement, Perpendicular.

Porches as early as those at Weston and West Walton are uncommon, but there is another thirteenth-century one at Bottisham, this time at the west end of the church instead of in the more usual position adjacent to one of the aisles. Morton and Swaffham Prior (St Mary) also have western porches. At Donington and Wisbech the once detached towers now serve as entrance porches to the church.

Some of the grander and later porches have two storeys, with the upper part accessible by a spiral staircase. At Boston, the upper room is open to the church and houses a parish library of nearly 1,200 books, including many printed in the sixteenth and seventeenth centuries. At Mildenhall and Fordham, the Lady Chapels occupy the upper parts of the north porches—a most unusual arrangement, particularly that at Fordham, since the chapel there is only accessible from outside the church.

Doors and Windows

Facing the visitor in the porch is the main doorway into the church. Before porches became common, this doorway was often a major architectural feature and several splendid examples of Norman and Early English doorways survive in Fenland parish churches.

There are round arches enclosing carved tympana at Peakirk and at Sempringham (north door). The tympanum at Peakirk has three fan motifs and is inside an arch ornamented with zig-zag and other designs; fan motifs also occur at Sempringham. But it is the south doorway at Sempringham that is the better known: here, three orders of shafts support a heavily moulded arch on capitals carved with leaves, again with zig-zag decoration. There are other good late twelfth-century doorways at Sutterton and Whaplode.

Towards the end of the Norman period, arches became pointed and decoration was extended to the shafts. Both are seen at Downham-in-the-Isle, where the south door incorporates the unusual motif of twenty-six tiny heads set along a roll moulding. There is another very late Norman doorway at Ely (St Mary) which combines unusual forms of zig-zag decoration on the arch with columns carrying shaft rings and stiff-leaf capitals which were to be a feature of the new (Early English) style. The aisle doorways at Kirton-in-Holland also demonstrate this transition from Norman to Early English work.

To see fully Early English doorways at their best, the visitor should go to Wrangle or to Elm, the north door at the latter having no fewer than seven orders of colonnettes supporting the finely moulded arches. Then about 1300, doorways in parish churches became less ornate, though there were occasional exceptions such as the trefoil-headed openings at Pinchbeck and Spalding (north door), as the artistic efforts of the masons were diverted to other parts of the building.

For the next eighty years, window tracery became a dominant decorative feature. The narrow lancet windows and bar tracery of the Early English period ceased to be fashionable and much larger openings filled with flamboyant tracery were incorporated in new work. This fashion was nowhere in Britain less restrained than in the Fenland. As Sir Nikolaus Pevsner has pointed out (*The Buildings of England: Lincolnshire* pp 39–43), the designers of these windows showed remarkable inventiveness while at the same time making use of quite a small number of standard elements: the ogee arch, the dagger and the mouchette.

The tracery of the earliest Decorated windows was at least partly geometrical in form. There are examples from this period at Billingborough and Rippingale (where the geometrical forms are uncommonly large) and include the five-light east window at Fishtoft and the very unusual east window at Mildenhall.

The windows at the west end of Swaton church are good examples of reticulated tracery, a form in which ogee arches are the sole elements. Among the many examples of flowing tracery, Heckington is once again superb, especially the seven-light east window and the five-light south transept south window. Other particularly fine windows are to be seen at Cambridge (Little St Mary's), Algakirk (though over-restored), Wisbech, Fenstanton, Yaxley, Watlington and Sutterton.

By the end of the fourteenth century, vertical elements began to predominate. The east window at Sutton-in-the-Isle and the ground floor tower windows at Holbeach show the beginnings of the Perpendicular style and it is seen in its maturity in the great east and west windows (of nine and eleven lights respectively) at King's Lynn (St Nicholas), in the west window at King's Lynn (St Margaret's), in several windows at Boston, and at Tattershall, where the heavy tracery and the preference for triangles rather than arches indicates that the wheel of fashion had almost turned full circle.

Nave and aisles

Inside the church, the visitor's immediate attention is likely to be focused on the arcade of the nave: the piers, their capitals and the arches which they support. The design of arcades inevitably paralleled the changes in fashion which we have already described for doors and windows, but on a larger scale and with a closer relationship to progress in the technology of building.

The transition from the earliest Norman work to the purity of Early English took place in stages. Piers, initially squat, as at Bicker, Sempringham and Cambridge (Holy Sepulchre), became more slender, notably at Thurlby, sometimes with round and octagonal piers alternating as at Walsoken (Pl 17, p 139). The basically square capitals became more ornate as time went on, scallops increasing in number and then giving way to waterleaf carving (eg Walsoken and Whaplode). Arches developed from simple forms such as the single steps at Tilney All Saints and Long Sutton to the mature style with zig-zag decoration at Walsoken.

Early English arcades are characterised by piers with detached shafts, by capitals carved with leaves in the form known as stiff-leaf and by finely moulded pointed arches. West Walton has one of the finest Early English interiors in Britain. The piers in the nave are circular with four detached Purbeck marble shafts (some have been renewed in wood) with shaft rings and carry capitals with high quality stiff-leaf carving; in the chancel the piers have eight such shafts each. The arches are very finely moulded and in the spandrels are painted shields in circular surrounds. The aisles were later widened and two large buttresses were erected at the west end, with the result that the exterior no longer matches the style of the detached tower as it did when first built (a drawing inside the church shows the original appearance).

Weston, too, has detached shafts (though the piers on the south side are octagonal) and excellent stiff-leaf capitals, while at Skirbeck and Wainfleet St Mary the shafts are set in hollows in an octagonal core. Moulton is earlier and here the shafts are not fully round and are still attached to the core. At Morton, the carved capitals are particularly naturalistic, resembling ferns.

In the fourteenth and fifteenth centuries, capitals became less ornate, and were usually circular or polygonal in form with horizontal mouldings; the castellated capitals at Donington are a variation on this theme, while the leaves, heads and animals at West Keal hark back to the earlier tradition. In the Perpendicular style, capitals were smaller or omitted altogether, so that the shafts of the piers continued upwards into the mouldings of the arches with little or no break in design; piers were now usually quatrefoil in section.

The arcades at Holbeach and Walpole St Peter stand out among fourteenth-century work and there are superb fifteenth-century arcades at Tattershall, King's Lynn (St Nicholas), Burwell and Cambridge (Great St Mary's), the walls of the latter two being filled with ornate blank tracery carved in clunch.

Clerestories

The row of openings above the arcade provides the means of lighting the nave in an aisled church. They became common in parish churches during the thirteenth century, although there are a few earlier examples such as the Norman one at Bicker and the late Norman ones at Whaplode and Long Sutton, the latter now being wholly inside the present church. In these three early clerestories, the rhythm of the narrow openings is enhanced by blank arcading on the outside, and the same is true of the Early English clerestory at West Walton, which also has blank arcading inside the church, though following a different pattern.

As narrow lancets gave way to Decorated or Perpendicular windows of two or three lights each, glass became the dominant feature of the clerestory and the scope for ornamental stonework decreased correspondingly. So we get long sequences of identical lights, such as the fourteen windows at Boston, Holbeach and Terrington St Clement (where they are arranged in pairs), the thirteen at Walpole St Peter, or the twelve at Gedney and Kirton-in-Holland.

In some clerestories, windows alternate to provide a more complex rhythm. At Moulton there are round headed and wider windows, at Old Leake alternate windows are Decorated and Perpendicular in form and at Terrington St John circular windows are interposed between two-light windows of normal shape.

To let in yet more light, some later medieval builders inserted windows at the east end of the nave, over the chancel arch, though such windows were not often circular—nor so ornate—as the one at Burwell.

Because chapels at the side of the chancel are uncommon in Fenland churches, there was little need for clerestories over the chancel; Tilney All Saints and Leverton are exceptions. Spalding once had aisles to the transepts and oval windows of the corresponding clerestories may still be seen.

Roofs
East Anglia is famous for the quality of its medieval church roofs and many in the eastern part of the Fens

are as fine. There is a remarkable variety of forms, since tie-beams, arched braces, tie-beams on arched braces, hammer-beams and double hammer-beams may each occur on their own or may alternate with one of the other forms.

All provide ample scope for ornamentation, for traceried work in the spandrels of braces and hammer-beams and above tie-beams, for figures (usually angels) on the ends of the hammer-beams and elsewhere, and for decoration on the beams themselves and on the wall plates. Stone corbels which support wall posts and braces provide a further opportunity for ornamentation.

The double hammer-beam roof at March (St Wendreda) is famous. There are four tiers of angels: at the base of the wall posts, at the ends of each hammer-beam and in the centre of the collar-beams above them—a veritable galaxy of the heavenly host, superbly carved in the fifteenth century. There are more modest double hammer-beam roofs at Elm and Willingham. The roof at Tilney All Saints is almost a double hammer-beam but, on careful inspection, the upper hammers are seen to be false.

Single hammer-beams occur on their own at Spalding, though here there are angels on the principal rafters between the hammer-beams, and at Whaplode. Hammer-beams alternate with arched braces supported on figured stone corbels at Northwold and with tie-beams on arched braces at Pinchbeck.

Roofs supported by alternate hammer-beams and tie-beams without braces include those at Mildenhall, Lakenheath, Isleham, Landbeach, Soham, Hockwold, Methwold, Outwell and Upwell—a splendid group from which it is hard to select particular examples. The best thing is to see them all and form one's own opinion.

At Wiggenhall St Mary Magdalen, tie-beams alternate with short beams carrying figures and at Leverington, the tie-beams are ornamented with tracery and supported on carved corbels.

The great roof of King's Lynn (St Nicholas) has tie-beams on arched braces which rise from between pairs of vaulted stone niches with arched queen posts and traceried spandrels above them. At Somersham the braces continue right up to the ridge-piece and there are many carved bosses.

The low-pitched roofs at Burwell, Tattershall and Cambridge (Great St Mary's) are supported directly by arched braces and at Walpole St Peter and West Lynn, where the pitch is steeper, arched braces supporting the principal rafters direct alternate with tie-beams on arched braces.

So far only nave roofs have been described, but in some of these churches the roofs in the transepts and aisles are also fine pieces of craftmanship which in less well endowed parts of Britain would justify individual mention.

Chancels

As it was the practice (later enforced by law) for the rector to be responsible for the upkeep of the chancel and the parishioners for the rest of the church, chancels did not always match the nave etc, in size, style or quality. Some rectors, such as Richard de Potesgrave who built the chancel at Heckington, or William of Longthorne who did the same at Fenstanton, nobly fulfilled their responsibilities, but others did not, though rarely with such deplorable results as the complete collapse of the chancel at Tydd St Giles in the eighteenth century.

Fenland parish churches can nevertheless boast a number of very fine chancels, some built at the same time as the churches to which they belong and others added later by munificent benefactors. The two Early English examples at Weston and Cherry Hinton differ considerably in their details, but both rely for their effect on the overall treatment of the interior walls, with shafting, blank arcading and arches being used to link together the tall, narrow lancet windows.

There is also tall blank arcading on the side walls of the later chancels at Sutton-in-the-Isle and Wilburton, though by the fourteenth century the masons seemed less concerned with the treatment of the side walls and concentrated their attention on the east window, often the largest and most ornate in the church, and lavished their skills on the detailed stonework of piscina, sedilia, Easter sepulchre and tomb recesses. The chancels at Heckington, Leverton, Frampton and Fenstanton are of this period; those at Over, Swavesey and Walpole St Peter are a little later.

The chancel at Walpole St Peter is unusual in more than one respect. The altar is raised well above the floor of the church to allow the construction underneath of a north–south passage inside the churchyard. Also the stalls in the chancel have ornate stone canopies, linked to the piscina and sedilia by blank arcading.

There is one notable exception to the usual rectangular ground plan for chancels and that is a great rarity: the fourteenth-century polygonal apse at Bluntisham.

Chapels at the sides of the chancel are not common in Fenland churches, but there are a few particularly ornate ones which probably originated as chantry chapels. They include the vaulted one at Mildenhall—a fine example of the Early English style—the Decorated south chapel at Langtoft and Perpendicular ones at Maxey, Hacconby and Leverton.

The chapel attached to the chancel at Willingham church is a separate structure with a stone roof carried on elegant arches and may have been built for the use of the bishops of Ely on their journeys between Ely and Cambridge. The little polygonal building with two floors and a steep stone roof attached to the north-east corner of Long Sutton church was not a chapel but a vestry, though it is no longer used as such.

Most chancels incorporate a small priest's door; these

are not only attractive in themselves but often provide valuable evidence about the date of a chancel which has been much restored. Frampton and Rippingale are two particularly attractive examples.

Woodwork and Metalwork

The tradition of craftmanship that inspired the splendid roofs was also responsible for the quality of the medieval doors, benches, screens and other furnishings in wood and metal.

Doors have not often survived constant usage, and sometimes even attack at times when churches were being used as places of refuge, but there are a few good examples of traceried medieval doors in Lincolnshire churches. The elaborate fourteenth-century flowing tracery on the south door at Boston is especially fine and there is an unusual door at Gedney which incorporates a wicket door with a small French ivory of the Crucifixion set in it; both main door and wicket door bear inscriptions and are ornamented with buttresses decorated with pellets or ball-flower. Metalwork on doors also gave scope for ornamentation, as the thirteenth-century iron scrollwork on the doors at Market Deeping and Sempringham and the medieval bronze doorknockers at Warboys and Boston demonstrate.

Wooden medieval lecterns are even rarer but there is one at Bury, near Ramsey, decorated with ogee-headed arcading, quatrefoils, oakleafs and acorns, and a wooden eagle lectern at Leverington. Noble brass eagle lecterns of the types made in East Anglia around 1500 are to be found in seven Fenland churches as well as in Peterborough cathedral; such lecterns were highly regarded, and two travelled as far as Italy where they are in the cathedrals at Urbino and Venice. More unusual is what is thought to be a Dutch seventeenth-century lectern at Landbeach, which supports the Bible on the outstretched wings of a seated angel.

117

PARISH CHURCHES AND CHAPELS

The churches along the eastern fen edge are remarkable for their large sets of medieval or Tudor benches with openwork traceried backs and for their splendidly carved bench ends. Those at Wiggenhall St Mary and Wiggenhall St Germans are famous, both for the completeness and quality of their sets of benches and above all for their bench ends which contain figures of saints in ornamented niches surmounted by large poppyheads flanked by smaller seated figures. Poppyheads elsewhere are not always of the usual fleur-de-lys design, but may be figures of people or animals and in several churches there are carved beasts etc on the armrests. Across the other side of the fens, the church at Swaton possesses a particularly fine set of fifteenth-century traceried bench ends.

There is a large set of stalls in the chancel at Boston, such as one finds in cathedrals and Cambridge college chapels. They date from 1390 and have an amusing collection of misericords under the seats; the canopies were added in the nineteenth century.

No particular part of the Fenland has a monopoly of good medieval screens: there are excellent fourteenth-century parclose screens at Bottisham and Willingham, a dainty two-storey screen of unusual design at Walsoken and the coving of the rood loft at Rippingale. Medieval pulpits are rare, but there is one in the chancel at Tattershall displaying finely traceried Perpendicular work.

There was a second flowering of craftmanship in wood during the seventeenth century. Many pulpits date from that period as it was then that the sermon became an important part of the service. There is an especially ornate Jacobean pulpit at Runcton Holme and an unusual one at Over with an ogee-shaped domed tester.

The finest collection of Jacobean woodwork is at Walpole St Peter (Pl 4, p 67). It includes a grand west screen with pediments and fluted pilasters around the openings into the nave and aisles, a spectacular font

118

cover which opens up to reveal paintings inside (there are others of these stunning constructions at Terrington St Clement and Wiggenhall St Mary), a notable pulpit and most of the seating.

Discussion of altar rails leads us away from woodwork and on to the Georgian period, from the striking Jacobean wooden rails at Isleham to the wrought iron rails at Boston, which, with the equally fine gates under the tower, were made about 1740. A number of churches retain large elegant Georgian chandeliers, two particularly fine examples being the three-tier ones at Frampton and Spalding.

Finally, movable furniture: there are traceried medieval chests at Wilton, Hacconby and Swaffham Bulbeck, the latter probably Italian in origin, and several churches near the Wash possess hudds, those curious graveside shelters to protect the priest at funerals (though we make no claim for them as fine woodwork!).

Stone Furnishings
The small church at Witcham is one of the few in the east of England to boast a medieval stone pulpit; it is Perpendicular work with blank cusped arches around the sides. Stone screens are almost as uncommon, the only Fenland examples being Lord Cromwell's elaborate rood screen at Tattershall and the much simpler Perpendicular one at Bottisham. At Emneth and Quadring there are attractively ornamented remnants of the rood stairs, but no screens.

Medieval fonts, on the other hand, have survived in large numbers. There are specially good Early English examples at Lakenheath and Weston (with shafts and stiff-leaf decoration) and Perpendicular ones at Leverington, Walsoken, Great Hale, Holbeach and Morton; the octagonal bowls, and often the stems, are richly carved with shields, figures, Instruments of the Passion, the sacraments and other items.

The white marble font in Prickwillow church is most unexpected. The bowl is decorated with shells, the heads of cherubs and beads of pearls, and the stem with acanthus leaves. It came from Ely cathedral, to which it was presented in 1693.

The fittings in chancels are more delicate and lack the robustness of fonts. Sedilia (triple canopied seats for priests) and piscina (bowls in which sacred vessels are washed) are commonly built into south walls, their arches matching those of doors and windows of the period. Plain Norman sedilia, such as the one at Horbling, are rare and were succeeded by much more ornate examples with miniature vaults and carved bosses, like those at Chesterton and Conington. The sedilia and piscina at Heckington are especially ornate and form, with the Easter sepulchre and the cusped tomb recess opposite, a group which is justly famous. The Easter sepulchre consists of a relatively small triangle-headed recess surrounded by figures carved in relief inside triangle-headed panels arranged in a pattern reminiscent of a cross-section of an aisled church with a crypt beneath. There are other ornate Easter sepulchres at Frampton and Northwold, the latter unfortunately damaged.

Monuments and Sculpture
The church at Fletton—now a part of Peterborough—is renowned for the remarkable series of intricate small Saxon carvings of figures and interlace work incorporated into the buttresses at the east end of the chancel. They are thought to date from the first half of the ninth century (and so are contemporary with the Hedda Stone in Peterborough cathedral) and probably formed part of. a frieze; indeed, they may have come from the Anglo-Saxon Peterborough Abbey, burnt down in 1116.

Fletton also has two Norman figures of saints inside the church, while at the little church of Wentworth in the Isle of Ely there is a carving of a priest which can be identified as late twelfth-century work from the architectural motifs that surround it.

There is a later figure of a priest, this time in Purbeck marble, at West Walton. A small carving of two arms holding a heart at Yaxley commemorates a heart burial, probably of William of Yaxley, Abbot of Thorney, who died in 1293. Other interesting thirteenth-century monuments are of a deacon holding open a book at Rippingale—a very rare type, matched by only two others in England—and a noble figure of a young Franciscan tertiary at Conington.

Conington has much to offer the student of church monuments, for here, in addition to a long series of Cotton monuments, of which the finest is that to Sir Robert (†1631) whose famous collection of manuscripts is now in the British Museum, there are monuments to King David and Prince Henry of Scotland, once lords of the manor. Other churches rich in monuments are Bottisham, Isleham, Landwade (more Cottons), Stow Bardolph (in the Jacobean Hare chapel), Wisbech, Spilsby and Oxborough.

Spilsby, a market town standing on the southern escarpment of the Lincolnshire wolds, but commanding a wide view over the northern fens, is notable for the Willoughby and Bertie monuments in the church, of which the most remarkable is that to Richard Bertie (†1582) and his wife Baroness Willoughby de Eresby (†1580)—an ostentatious and conceited piece. Equally famous and elaborate, but far more graceful, are the Bedingfeld monuments at Oxborough, made of terracotta in a groping Renaissance style about 1525.

Other notable monuments need to be sought out individually, the most important being the fourteenth-century effigy of Sir Humphrey Littlebury at Holbeach, the incised marble slab to a Hanseatic merchant (†1340) at Boston, Colonel Edmund Soames (†1706) at West Dereham, Lady Cutt (†1631) at Swavesey, the ten-poster to Sir Anthony and Lady Irby (††1610, 1625) at

Whaplode, the tablet by Rysbrack to Sigismond Trafford (†1741) at Tydd St Mary, and Sir Thomas Hewar and his wife by Nicholas Stone (1617) at Emneth.

Brasses

The Fenland is rich in high quality medieval brasses, several of which date from the fourteenth century. The two splendid brasses at King's Lynn (St Margaret's) have already been mentioned and others of comparable quality are to be found at Isleham (Thomas Peyton †1484, with two fashionably dressed wives under ornate canopies), Wisbech (Thomas de Braunstone †1401), Sawtry (Sir William le Moyne †1404 and wife, with animals etc), Methwold (Sir Adam de Clifton †1367, unfortunately incomplete), Boston (Walter Pescod †1398 and wife, and other brasses), Gedney (a lady of about 1400 with a puppy, incomplete) and several at Tattershall.

Wall Paintings

Wall paintings in Fenland parish churches do not compare in either quality or completeness with those at Longthorpe Tower (see p 154). The most interesting set is at Peakirk, where there is a St Christopher, a number of scenes of the Passion, including the rarely-featured miracle of Longinus, and the Living and the Dead in which the element of decay is powerfully represented in a background of insects feeding on putrefaction. Other reasonably well preserved wall paintings are at Willingham, Chippenham, Yaxley, Friskney and Lakenheath.

Glass

Very little of the medieval glass in Fenland parish churches escaped the attentions of the iconoclasts in the seventeenth century. Apart from small fragments in window heads, there are remains of Jesse windows at Leverington and Gedney, a complete fifteenth-century window with figures of the Virgin and the Resurrection at Wistow, two complete fourteenth-century figures in the now disused church at Wood Walton, a dismounted figure of a knight in armour at Long Sutton and an almost complete Resurrection and other figures at Wrangle. Of these the Jesse window at Leverington is perhaps the most interesting since 13 of the original 61 figures survive and another 17 have been restored; they are all in oval medallions joined by vine scrolls.

Most of the late fifteenth-century stained glass at Tattershall was removed in the eighteenth century and taken to Stamford where it is now in St Martin's Church and Burghley House; it is sadly missed since Tattershall church does so desperately need colour to soften its hard lines.

All Saints, Jesus Lane, Cambridge and the parish church at Doddington both contain early stained glass by Morris and Co from the period when Morris himself, Burne-Jones and Ford Madox Brown were the designers. It is a pleasure to find some attractive modern glass at Spalding and Weston in soft subdued colours which tone with their medieval surroundings; the artist is H W Harvey of York.

Later Fenland Churches and Chapels

Not all Fenland churches are medieval and, as the fens were drained, churches were provided to meet the needs of the new populations. They include a simple chapel at Guyhirne, bearing the date 1660, and the octagonal Moulton Chapel built in 1722 by the elder William Sands in a Dutch style and to which a chancel has since been added.

An early eighteenth-century church at North Runcton, near King's Lynn, was probably designed by Henry Bell, the architect of the Customs House and other buildings in Lynn itself. The square nave has a central dome-shaped vault supported on four columns, with big arched windows in line with it. The chancel was added in 1894.

The draining of the fens north and west of Boston in

PARISH CHURCHES AND CHAPELS

the nineteenth century led to the building of chapels at
Midville, Eastville, Frithville and Wildmore under the
provisions of the Fen Chapels Act 1812. Though differing
considerably in size and details, these are all in the
classical style reminiscent of the work of Jeptha Pacey,
the architect of the church at Whaplode Drove.

There was another spate of church building in the
second half of the nineteenth century in the Holbeach
area. Again, the designs have much in common: several
churches having little or no structural division between
nave and chancel, open timber-framed roofs, lancet
windows and Gothic-style benches. Churches were being
built, too, all over the Cambridgeshire fens at the same
time.

Victorian churches built in the expanding towns are
unexceptional apart from Bodley's All Saints, Cambridge, with its wealth of pre-Raphaelite stained glass
and decoration.

The nineteenth century was also a period of great
activity in the building of non-conformist chapels, and
there is at least one in most of the larger villages and in
the towns. It is hard to be enthusiastic about the
architectural quality of most of those in the Fens: too
often they are rather overpowering box-like buildings
constructed in 'white' brick, which probably looked
more attractive when sketched on an architect's drawing
board than they do standing in a village street.

There are, of course, exceptions and one is doubly
pleased to discover such buildings as the Unitarian
Chapel of 1819 in Spain Lane, Boston, with segment-
headed windows of an attractive design that recurs
elsewhere in the town, the red-brick Methodist chapel
at Whaplode with its Gothic windows and another at
East Keal which remains classical in style though built
as late as 1863. Any searcher after the unusual will not
want to miss the Neo-Egyptian façade to the Free-
mason's Hall in Boston, modelled on the portico of the
Temple of Dandour in Nubia.

124

7 Fenland Towns and Villages

FENLAND towns fall easily into three groups. There are the ports which ring the Wash and stand on the estuaries of the main rivers though, owing to reclamation, each is now several miles from the sea. Then there are the small market towns inside the Fenland, some of which grew up outside the gates of the medieval monasteries. Finally, where the rivers and their tributaries descend from the higher ground towards the Fenland, towns of strategic importance exist where the ancient roads cross the rivers; of these, only Peterborough actually stands on the fen edge, but the history of all of them is bound up with that of the Fens.

There was no settlement in the Fenland having the status of a borough at the time of the Domesday survey. King's Lynn and Boston were founded shortly after and Sleaford was established on a new site near the castle being built by Alexander, Bishop of Lincoln. These were 'plantation towns', the medieval equivalent of the 'new towns' of today. A fourth such town, established at Holme in the twelfth century, did not survive, though it was a parliamentary borough until the passing of the First Reform Act in 1832.

Other Fenland towns grew up and became rich during the thirteenth and fourteenth centuries on the profits of the wool trade and, by 1334, most of them were to be numbered among the hundred richest places in England. Thereafter, in Tudor times, wool exports decreased, but

King's Lynn, with its large trading hinterland, maintained its prosperity as that of other towns declined.

The draining of the Fens led to an increase in trade along the improved rivers and there was a further period of prosperity during the later seventeenth century and the eighteenth century. The two main periods of prosperity are reflected in the architecture of the towns: the medieval churches and guildhalls and the Georgian warehouses, hotels and domestic buildings.

The Medieval Ports

King's Lynn is the richest of the Fenland ports in its medieval remains and the town still retains its medieval plan. The earliest settlement was probably in South Lynn and it was to the north of this that Bishop Herbert de Losinga's monastic town grew up around St Margaret's Priory (see p 93) early in the twelfth century. There followed the building of a new town north of the Purfleet, with its own market place (the Tuesday market) and chapel of St Nicholas.

A survey of three houses on the east side of King Street made by the Norfolk Archaeological Unit in 1974 led to the exciting discovery that there was a Norman house embedded inside the present walls. The architectural details suggest that it must have been built about 1200 and is therefore almost certainly one of the original houses of the new town.

Early in the fifteenth century, the residential and commercial area along Nelson Street and Queen Street was established on land reclaimed from the river. Hampton Court in Nelson Street is an almost complete group of a merchant's buildings, with shops facing the street, hall, parlour, service rooms and counting house along one side of the courtyard behind and warehouses facing the river (Pl 9). The warehouses on the north side, which close the courtyard, were added about 1600 and probably replaced a range contemporary with the earlier buildings.

Clifton House in Queen Street has a medieval undercroft and a fourteenth-century pavement of Clare tiles which may well be the most substantial secular pavement of its date in England. Behind the house is an Elizabethan brick lookout tower and a complex of warehouses dating from that period.

Among other medieval secular buildings are the warehouses of the steelyard built by the Hanseatic merchants in St Margaret's Lane, the so-called Hanseatic warehouse on South Quay and the two guildhalls, both of which date from the fifteenth century. The front of the Guildhall of the Holy Trinity in the Saturday Market is a much-photographed essay in flint and stone chequer-work which now forms part of a group of public buildings of different periods, the others being the gaol, the assembly rooms and the town hall. St George's Guildhall, in King Street, is the largest surviving medieval guildhall in England; it has recently been restored and is now a theatre and concert hall.

Other fragments of the medieval town include sections of the wall to be seen on the east and north sides of the town, the South Gate standing across London Road, the Greyfriars tower and the curious Red Mount Chapel.

By comparison with those of King's Lynn, the medieval remains in the other Fenland ports are scanty. Apart from its magnificent church, Boston has only the Guildhall of the Blessed Virgin Mary (now a museum) and the Blackfriars Hall, recently given a new lease of life as an arts centre. There was a Hanseatic steelyard at Boston as well as at Lynn, an indication of the importance of these two ports in medieval times, but nothing of it remains today.

In Spalding, there is Ayscoughee Hall, part of which betrays its origin as a brick country house of 1429, since engulfed by the town and now mostly a mixture of Elizabethan and Victorian rebuilding, and the Abbey Buildings which were perhaps part of the priory.

Of medieval Wisbech, virtually nothing remains apart

from the parish church and the town plan. Wainfleet All Saints has even lost its medieval parish church, but it makes up for it by the school, founded in 1484 by William Waynflete, Bishop of Winchester. This rather stolid brick building, now the public library, is in the tradition of Tattershall Castle and may well have been designed by John Cowper who was working for Bishop Waynflete on Tattershall Church at the same time.

The Ports in the Seventeenth Century and the Georgian Period

It is the work of Henry Bell at King's Lynn which most forcibly expresses the revolution in architectural styles which occurred in the seventeenth century—the contrast between the vernacular Greenland Fisheries Building of 1605 and Bell's Customs House of 1683 is complete. Irregular timber framing has given way to wrought stone, perfect symmetry, regular curves and classical motifs.

Henry Bell was a self-taught architect, whose buildings are characterised by a fine sense of scale and by their inventiveness. In addition to the Customs House he was responsible for the Duke's Head Hotel, with its dominating broken pediment, and the façade of Clifton House, unusual in Britain for the barley-sugar columns which flank the doorway.

Although King's Lynn is not lacking in good Georgian houses, particularly in King Street, it lacks that juxta-position of Georgian buildings and river which are the glories of Wisbech and Spalding. It is characteristic of these riverside streets that the grander houses, the cottages of the artisans and the commercial buildings all blend happily together, being built of similar materials and sharing a common sense of scale.

Thus North Brink at Wisbech, which begins as one of the finest Georgian streets in England, continues as a road of smaller houses and ends with a brewery.

Indeed, the early eighteenth-century warehouse among the row of stately Georgian town houses seems more at home there than do the gabled nineteenth-century houses further along the street.

At Spalding, houses, warehouses and cottages jostle each other along the riverside, an arrangement which no new town planner would propose today; yet how convenient it must have been! The riverside here lacks the stateliness of the Brinks at Wisbech, but it makes up for it by its greater variety, its more intimate scale and the trees on either side of the river. Moreover, the river at Spalding is no longer tidal as the main channel has been diverted to the east of the town, so that the water level does not fall to reveal the piling and the grey mud as the Nene does at Wisbech.

There is no individual house at Spalding to compare with Peckover House at Wisbech or Fydell House at Boston, but there are many very pleasant groups by the river and near the church, including the terrace of ten houses in London Road known as Welland Terrace. The best individual house is probably Holland House, built in 1768 by the younger William Sands, who was also responsible for Langton House and Westbourne Lodge in Cowbit Road. The two William Sands, father and son, were local masons-cum-architects whose style is characterised chiefly by its wealth of Palladian motifs, sometimes crammed uncomfortably close together.

Fydell House in South Square, Boston, exemplifies these characteristics and may perhaps have been the work of William Sands, senior. There is good woodwork and plaster work inside, but nothing to compare with the extraordinary richness of Peckover House, in spite of the comparative simplicity of the latter's exterior. Peckover House was built in 1722 and the staircase and most of the decoration dates from then, but the plaster-work at the head of the stairs and the overmantel above the fireplace in the drawing room must be later as their mature rococo style is that of the middle of the eighteenth century. The garden is unexpectedly large for a town house and contains one of the largest maidenhair trees in the country; three orange trees fruit regularly in the conservatory.

The other important Georgian development in Wisbech is on the Castle estate. In the centre stood the original Norman castle and, later, Secretary Thurloe's house, also known as Wisbech Castle, of which a contemporary painting hangs in Peckover House (see p 159). Around this a local builder, Joseph Medworth, built the Crescent and the corresponding buildings on the north side of the castle garden early in the nineteenth century. Nearby is a gabled seventeenth-century house of brick with stone dressings, which may also have been built by Secretary Thurloe.

Boston's Georgian inheritance is more scattered and there is nothing comparable to the riverside terraces at Wisbech and Spalding. A few early nineteenth-century houses face the Witham above the Grand Sluice and, at the south end of the town, Georgian houses overlook the river across the busy London Road. In between there are several Georgian façades in the High Street, the most notable being number 120. To the east of the river are squares and other groups of eighteenth and early nineteenth-century houses. Even quite small cottages often have good doorcases but many are, alas, in a sad condition.

Apart from Fydell House and the nearby Customs House of 1725, most of the larger houses are in Wide Bargate, the second of the two market places in the town. In the Market Place itself, facing the church, are the impressive Exchange Buildings—fifteen bays crowned with a pediment bearing the town's arms and the date 1772—and the assembly rooms of 1826.

The Peacock and Royal Hotel, the interior of which contained examples of artisan mannerism (see p 159) behind a later Georgian facade, has unfortunately been demolished and Boston no longer has a market place hostelry to compare with the Duke's Head at King's Lynn, the White Hart at Spalding or the Rose and Crown at Wisbech.

One is concerned, too, about the future of the Georgian warehouses at the four ports. Many of these noble buildings have already been demolished and others appear neglected. There are some particularly good examples opposite Fydell House at Boston: buildings four or five storeys high and about 14 bays in length backing on to the river. It is to be hoped that a use will continue to be found for the best of them.

Spalding also has a quite different claim to fame as the home of the oldest antiquarian society in Britain. The Spalding Gentlemen's Society was founded in 1709–10 and, although its objects were not solely antiquarian, the presence among the early members of William Stukeley (a native of Holbeach) and others with similar interests, gave it a strong bias in that direction.

The Ports Today

Boston and King's Lynn are still significant ports, with over 1,000 ships entering or leaving each during the year to discharge or load foodstuffs, timber, fuels and manufactured goods, much of the trade being with Scandinavian, Baltic and EEC ports. At both ports, ships can lie afloat in enclosed docks entered from the river through locks. They are well equipped with facilities for handling container traffic and King's Lynn also has facilities for handling roll-on/roll-off traffic. In 1973, Boston handled 837,000 tonnes of cargo and King's Lynn 887,000 tonnes. In the same year, 213,000 tonnes of cargo was handled at Wisbech; here ships berth in the river just as they did in the middle years of the nineteenth century when a local owner, Richard Young, operated a fleet of 15 or 20 ships from the port.

It is King's Lynn which, to the modern visitor, presents the greatest contrasts, with its grain elevators

131

and medieval warehouses jostling each other along the quay, Georgian and medieval buildings in the Nelson Street–Queen Street–King Street area and then, in the traffic-free High Street, the shops one finds in every town in Britain. Outside this core area there has been much demolition and new building, the whole presenting an image in keeping with that of a town bent on expansion and on receiving industry and workpeople moving away from the Greater London area. To the other ports, change comes more slowly, though not always more happily.

In particular, Wisbech, situated roughly mid-way between the expanding towns of Peterborough and King's Lynn, has not shared in their growth and finds it hard to compete with them as an employment, shopping or entertainment centre. Its problems are described in one of the small town studies undertaken by the East Anglia Consultative Committee (*Small Town Studies*, Cambridge, 1972) and stem largely from too heavy a dependence on agriculture and food processing, both industries which still involve substantial amounts of casual and seasonal employment.

Market Towns

The five ports are also market towns where official markets are held on one or more days each week. Such markets were more common in medieval times in spite of the smaller population, since they then provided almost the only means by which the country people sold their produce and purchased the things which they could not make or grow for themselves. The number of markets reached a peak in the thirteenth century and then declined; some were not revived after the Black Death and others died a natural death as improved communications rendered them less necessary. Even so, new ones continued to come into existence, one at Earith being founded as late as 1623.

In the relatively sparsely populated Fenland, the area served by a market in Elizabethan times was 100 square miles or more. There were then markets in several communities which have since reverted to the status of villages: Kirton-in-Holland, Crowland, Donington, Tattershall, Reach, Earith, Yaxley, Soham, Methwold and (though we shall mention it here) Market Deeping. Also, among the smaller towns, Ramsey and Littleport no longer have markets.

Whittlesey is one of the pleasantest Fenland market towns. The central Market Place, around the Butter Cross, retains its eighteenth-century character and spaciousness and the 'multiples' with their standardised shopfronts have so far been successfully excluded. Nearby, a secluded open space has been created by clearing the graveyard in front of the splendid spire of St Mary's church, though one cannot but regret the removal of some of the fine headstones shown in older photographs (see, for example, Pl 86 in Alec Clifton-Taylor's *English Parish Churches*). A little further away are a number of new developments, their scale in keeping with that of the older parts of the town and each having a unity of its own. The existence of two medieval parish churches in a town the size of Whittlesey is unusual; both are still in use.

March is dominated by the railway, even in the post-Beeching era, and the sharply curving platforms with their pitched roofs orientated *across* the platform are a familiar sight to East Anglian railway travellers. North of the station are the mechanised Whitemoor marshalling yards, among the largest in Britain and a hive of activity in spite of British Rail's relative lack of interest in wagon-load consignments. The church of St Wendreda, with its superb angel roof, is over a mile away at the southern edge of the town; this was the site of the original settlement, before river traffic led to the building of the town where it is now.

Ely is still very much a city of the fens, centred

around the great abbey which originally brought it into being and meeting essentially local needs, just as it did in medieval times. There are no grandiose plans for expansion and it is still many miles from the motorway network. It is, however, surprisingly well served by trains and is an important interchange station, with regular through services to Manchester, Birmingham, Doncaster, Norwich, Harwich and London.

The river, too, brings its quota of visitors in summer and the river frontage is one of the pleasantest parts of the town, extending from the Georgian Cutter Inn past the nineteenth-century Maltings, now a hall for concerts and other activities, to an attractive grouping of eighteenth-century cottages facing the former commercial quay.

The cathedral dominates the higher ground. Facing the west end, across the Palace Green, are two fine eighteenth-century houses and the parish church of St Mary and its vicarage, the latter a half-timbered building which Oliver Cromwell inherited and made his home before the Civil War.

The business of the town is still mainly agricultural—the market, the sugar beet factory, the suppliers of farm machinery and fertilisers—though tourism has grown steadily in recent years.

Further east, where the river Lark enters the fens, is Mildenhall. Opposite the church, in the centre of the town, is the Market Place with an hexagonal market cross built of timber in the sixteenth century. Behind the older houses of the Market Place is a pleasant modern shopping centre, though old and new buildings could be better appreciated if the town were rather less overrun by large motor cars. By the river are the remains of a port with quays and warehouses and an unusually large watermill. The nearby airfield was the starting point for the England–Australia air race in 1934.

On the western fen edge, on the line of the ancient

Mareham Lane, are Bourne and Market Deeping. Bourne's attraction lies in a number of individual buildings, especially the Free School of 1678, Red Hall and the Town Hall of 1821, with its horseshoe staircase recessed behind a screen of Doric columns. In its restoration of Red Hall, a Jacobean mansion of brick with an ornate two-storey stone porch and its adaptation as a community centre, the local council has set an example which others would do well to emulate. Market Deeping, on the other hand, makes its impact as a whole. Here wide streets of pleasant stone buildings, many in the style that is associated with nearby Stamford, meet at the former market place.

There is not space to do more than list the remaining Fenland market towns: Holbeach on the silt ridge south of the Wash, Downham Market in the carstone district of Norfolk, and Ramsey and Chatteris on their islands in the fen to the west of Ely.

Peterborough

Peterborough, like Ely and Ramsey, was a market town which grew up outside the gates of a great abbey. The completion of the Great Northern Railway in 1852 made it an important junction on the east coast main line and a few years later began the exploitation for brickmaking of the bed of Oxford clay to the south and east of the town. Other industrial development followed and has been continuous ever since.

The city is now bent on expansion and a vast modern housing estate is springing up to the west. Of the city's historic past, there is little to be seen beyond the cathedral, the parish church of St John the Baptist, the seventeenth-century Guildhall in the Market Place and a few scattered Georgian houses, the best of which are in Priestgate. There was an important prehistoric and Roman settlement at Fengate on the eastern edge of the city, which has recently been excavated (see p 21).

The city is now incorporated in the enlarged county of Cambridgeshire and vies with Huntingdon and Cambridge as an administrative centre.

Cambridge

Is Cambridge a Fenland town? To the inhabitants of Cottenham, Landbeach and a host of other Fenland villages, Cambridge is their market town. On the other hand, to the foreign tourists who crowd King's Parade each summer, Cambridge is the university and colleges; *their* interest in the town is probably confined to the contents of the antique shops and the menus of the cafes.

Town and gown have lived in an uneasy partnership for seven centuries and each owes a great deal to the other: the town is adorned by the more elegant of the college and university buildings and by the gardens, inspired by the Fitzwilliam and many smaller museums, and enlivened by the concerts and plays which it would not otherwise be able to support, while the university is utterly dependent on the services provided by the townspeople.

The town, on the other hand, did exist for thirteen centuries before that historic migration by a group of Oxford scholars took place in 1209. The earliest substantial settlement was that of the Iron Age Belgic peoples, traces of which have been excavated on Castle Hill. To the Romans, Cambridge was an important strategic centre: it marked the crossing place of two major roads (Worstead Street and Akeman Street) and was the head of navigation on the river Cam. The Roman camp on Castle Hill was a rectangular earthwork at the intersection of the two roads.

The Anglo-Saxons, too, established a settlement there, but there were other Saxon settlements in Newnham, Barnwell and the area around St Bene'ts Church. The latter seems to have developed as the commercial centre and in the tenth century we read of Irish merchants in

136

the town, evidence that Cambridge was already an inland port, carrying on trade with overseas as well as with other British ports.

The Normans followed and, in building their castle, they destroyed part of the Saxon settlement on Castle Hill. By then the market area to the south-east of the river had established itself as the dominant part of the town and was already large enough to support several churches, though only St Bene'ts contains a substantial amount of Saxon work today. The grant of a charter and the establishment of Stourbridge Fair on the meadows to the north of the town about 1200 consolidated the position of Cambridge as an important borough.

By the end of the thirteenth century, during which the first scholars had arrived in Cambridge and the first college (Peterhouse) had been founded, the town could boast fifteen churches, a priory, a nunnery, two hospitals and the establishments of four or five orders of friars. Ten of the medieval churches still exist and fragments of some of the other buildings are incorporated in college buildings (in particular at Jesus College, see p 94). A rare survival is a Norman domestic building in the grounds of St John's College: the so-called School of Pythagoras, built about 1200, of clunch with ashlar dressings.

A second medieval domestic building survives in Chesterton. It is Chesterton Tower, built in the fourteenth century as the residence of the Procurator of the Abbot of Vercelli, on whom Chesterton church had been bestowed. Each floor forms one complete room, with octagonal turrets at the north and west corners and a garderobe projection on the south; the presence-chamber on the ground floor retains its original vault.

The medieval town on the east side of the river was bounded by King's Ditch, which swept round following the line of Mill Lane, Pembroke Street, Hobson Street and Park Street. The earliest colleges were built outside this area but later ones were within it, occupying sites by the river which cut one of the main streets of the town, fragments of which still exist in Queens' Lane and Trinity Lane. The first university, as opposed to college, buildings were not completed until about 1400 on the site behind the Senate House, which is now known as the Old Schools.

The relationship between the colleges and the university puzzles many visitors. Colleges are independent foundations, to one of which every undergraduate or graduate student must belong. They house a substantial proportion of their student members and undertake a limited amount of teaching. They also serve as social centres for members of the university staff who are elected into fellowships. The university, on the other hand, confers degrees, organises lectures and laboratory classes, and provides facilities for research work.

Neither town nor university grew very much between Elizabethan times and the beginning of the nineteenth century. Some colleges erected new buildings on their existing sites and the Senate House was built, but there was no increase in the number of undergraduates— indeed, there were fewer in 1800 than in 1600.

Then about 1800 all this changed: the university was reformed, a new desire for learning began to disperse the lethargy of the seventeenth and eighteenth centuries, and Downing, the first of a new generation of colleges, was founded. The town, too, began its expansion following the enclosure in 1807 of a large area of common land to the east and south-east of the market area. The story of this expansion is a complicated one (see, for example, G Taylor: *The Cambridgeshire Landscape*, pp 264–9). It resulted in the quadrupling of the population of Cambridge between 1800 and 1900 and accounts for the existence of so many nineteenth-century houses in those parts of the town.

The university expansion in the nineteenth century included the addition of new courts to existing colleges, the building of the Old University Library and the

Plate 17 The late-Norman nave at Walsoken on the edge of the Norfolk marshland. In the foreground is the splendid Perpendicular font with figures of the seven sacraments, crucifixion and saints (*Crown Copyright Reserved*)

Plate 18 (*above*) Speed skaters on Whittlesey Wash, with Dog-in-a-Doublet sluice in the background (*Cambridge Evening News*)

Plate 19 (*below*) Flooded washland at Welney. Here the grassland is used for summer grazing and scattered thorn bushes provide shelter for animals (*K. Sellers*)

Fitzwilliam Museum, the foundation of further colleges about 1870, including two for women, and the erection of the first of a long series of scientific laboratories. Expansion continued in the twentieth century, reaching a peak in the 1950's and the 1960's and spreading through the residential area of west Cambridge and on to the farmland beyond.

The importance of Cambridge as an inland port declined sharply after the railway arrived in 1845, although the growth of the town continued unabated. The villages of Barnwell, Chesterton, Cherry Hinton and Trumpington have been absorbed and beyond them a green belt gives a temporary breathing space before reaching the so-called 'necklace' villages, including some in the Fens, from which many workers commute daily into Cambridge.

Today, Cambridge is at the centre of a region containing several industrial, agricultural and government concerns producing chemicals, plastics, electronic equipment and instruments, some of which derived their initial inspiration from the presence of the university. 'Cambridge—the centre of scientific research' is a familiar advertising slogan which has considerable justification.

Cambridge Architecture

It is natural in discussing the buildings of Cambridge to think principally—or indeed, only—of the college and university buildings. Endless books have been written about them, from the great work by Willis and Clark down to the humblest guide book. Each age from the thirteenth century onwards has made its contribution and, since there was for long, general agreement over matters of size, scale and material, buildings of different styles almost always stand happily together. At least, this was so until the present century, when the wide range of materials available and the desperate desire of certain architects to do something different without any

141

apparent respect for tradition or for neighbouring buildings, has led to some mediocre and even plainly ugly work. One should not, however, underestimate the difficulties of building on confined sites in juxtaposition to buildings of more than one period, while at the same time satisfying the whims and budget imposed by a college or university committee.

But Cambridge as a Fenland town is primarily a town of houses, shops, public buildings and churches (mentioned in Chapter 6). The best place from which to get a general view of Cambridge is the top of the tower of Great St Mary's church. From it one sees the parklike 'backs' to the west, the Market Square with its gaily coloured canopies to the east, Castle Hill to the northwest and the narrow streets and jumbled roofs of the older buildings near at hand.

Cambridge is still well endowed with timber-framed houses, though in only a few of them is the frame any longer visible from the street. Most have been plastered over, but occasionally tiles have been used to protect the frame and infilling (eg 4 and 5 Market Hill and 32 Hobson Street) and several of what appear to be brick houses actually have timber frames (eg 22 King's Parade, facing Great St Mary's Church, and part of 12 Mill Lane).

The best pre-nineteenth century streets remaining in Cambridge are Bridge Street, Magdalene Street, Northampton Street, Trinity Street, King's Parade and Bene't Street. Here one can find substantial groups of vernacular or Georgian buildings on one side or other of the street but hardly ever on both. Magdalene Street has the best vernacular architecture and Trinity Street the best eighteenth-century houses, including some original shopfronts. In both these streets, colleges have sensitively adapted or rebuilt houses without affecting the street frontage. A few years ago, King Street would have been included in this list but redevelopment has utterly destroyed it.

The early nineteenth-century expansion is well represented in complete streets and groups of houses. Here one can cite Park Terrace (and what little remains of Parkside) facing Parker's Piece, Scroope Terrace and Bene't Place at the east end of Lensfield Road, and 8–18 Maid's Causeway among the larger houses and Fitzwilliam Street, Malcolm Street, New Square, Willow Walk, Tennis Court Terrace and Tennis Court Road among the smaller.

Another attractive feature is the groups of cottages which line narrow lanes in various parts of the town: St Edward's Passage, Botolph Lane, Little St Mary's Lane, Portugal Place, Orchard Street (a particularly charming curved row of 14 similar cottages with mansard roofs near New Square, built in 1825) and Malting Lane.

Apart from these groups and streets, there are many good individual houses and inns of various periods. In Trumpington Street alone there is the sixteenth-century Little Rose Inn, timber-framed with two gabled bays facing the street, the Peterhouse Master's Lodge, built in 1702 as a private house, in red brick with stone dressings, Fitzwilliam House (1727) and two late eighteenth-century houses in yellow brick: Kenmare with its four Venetian windows and Grove Lodge next to the Fitzwilliam Museum extension. Best of all, though, is 16 Jesus Lane, a five-bay, three-storey house in dark red brick with a central pediment and urns standing on the parapet. The staircase and panelling inside are original and there are two fireplaces of about 1760, one of which is elaborately carved in rococo style. Finally, a word of praise to British Rail for restoring the fifteen arches of the façade of the railway station to something approaching their original appearance and at the same time making good use of the space behind them.

Fenland Villages

Villages derive their character from their situation, their shape or plan, and the materials and architectural styles in which they are built. In the Fenland, suitable situations are restricted to those which are immune to flooding, or at least are sufficiently far above the general flood level to escape it under normal conditions. Thus the villages are concentrated around the fen edge, on the silt ridge which describes an arc around the southern and western shores of the Wash, and on the islands of greensand or boulder clay which obtrude through the peat fen.

Benwick and Prickwillow do not fit into this pattern but are built on roddons, the silted-up channels of disused watercourses. Benwick is the older village: its main street was once the course of the West Water and the houses on either side have their foundations on the levees formed by that river. Some of the houses are leaning back from the street because the outer faces of the levees contain peat as well as silt and so form inadequate foundations. Prickwillow is on the roddon of the Ouse which originally followed a course to the east of the present artificial channel between Ely and Littleport.

Some characteristics are common to Fenland villages, whatever their location. Spaciousness is one of these; there is no need in the flat Fenland for buildings to be huddled together on top of one another, as they must be where they are confined within a narrow valley or between cliffs and sea. This spaciousness takes many forms: a wide main street as at Donington, Baston and Parson Drove, a combination of road and river running through the village, as at Bicker, Fen Drayton, Upwell, Outwell and Deeping Gate, or a central open space (pl 15, p 106).

Village greens are not, in fact, as uncommon in Fenland villages as some writers have suggested. Wicken, Moulton, Helpringham, Morton, Peakirk, Thorney, Walpole St Peter, Wimbotsham, Elm, Methwold, Rampton, Willingham, Haddenham and Waterbeach all have village greens of one kind or another.

Tattershall is built round a square which probably had its origins as a village green-cum-market place. Elsewhere the sense of spaciousness conferred by a village green arises from the presence of a centrally placed churchyard; Glinton and Kirton-in-Holland are good examples.

Another feature common to a great many low-lying Fenland villages is that the church, being the oldest and most important building, is built on the highest piece of land. In villages such as Yaxley, Sutton-in-the-Isle, Stretham or Horbling, the church dominates the scene and the houses and shops nestle or are strung out below it. More often, however, it will mean that it is only a few feet above the rest of the village, but since the church in many low-lying villages had to serve as a refuge in times of flood, those few feet may be critical. Again there are exceptions: at Runcton Holme the church is situated on the fenward side of the village street and other villages (Quadring, Wainfleet St Mary, Wood Walton) have their churches well away from the village.

With so much water about, it's not surprising that duckponds are a rarity: are Wicken, Soham and Billingborough the only examples?

Two of the most attractive Fenland villages are built around watercourses. At Bicker a stream winds through the village between grassy banks planted with trees; the scale is small and the trees and buildings—be they cottages, shops or church—close the short vista at a twist of the road. At Fen Drayton, a dyke lined with chestnut and ash runs along one side of the High Street, separating the street from the gardens of the brick and half-timbered houses on that side. Even the overhead electricity cables and the corrugated iron roofs on two of the cottages opposite are no more than unfortunate elements in an otherwise charming scene.

At Upwell and Outwell, the juxtaposition of waterway and buildings is less intimate. The roads on either side of the Old Nene, the Well Creek and the Wisbech Canal

145

are wider and busier and there are few trees. Crowland may have been similar before the river was diverted away from the incredible triangular bridge that now stands high and dry at the centre of the village.

The fen-edge villages fall into groups, differing in character as well as in the materials of which they are built. While the inhabitants of all of them no doubt made good use of the plentiful supplies of fish, fowl, sedge and turves available in the fen, some fen-edge villages seem to embrace the fen while others stand away from it. The villages along the northern edge of the fens are of the remote kind: they stand on the high ground of the Lincolnshire wolds or are separated from the fen edge by a belt of parkland. The same is true of some of the Norfolk fen-edge villages, but many of those to the west and south of the fens stand right on the fen edge with the village street strung out parallel to it, or less often, driving straight out into the fen. These are the real fen-edge villages.

Horbling is one of the most attractive of the villages on the western edge of the fens. The main street of mostly Georgian houses sweeps round in a gentle curve as it climbs up to the church. In Spring Lane, a shaded spring of crystal-clear water feeds a deep cistern and stone troughs, probably once used for washing when no other water supply was available.

For the villages along the southern and south-eastern fen-edges, the fenland waterways were channels for trade, along which they received coal, timber and manufactured goods, shipping in return the agricultural products of East Anglia.

Reach, for example, was a port in Roman times and there are records of trade through it from the fourteenth to the nineteenth centuries. The remains of the hythe and its basins can be traced today at the end of the rectangular green around which the village appears to be built. Originally there was no green, but two distinct villages separated by the Devil's Dyke; it was only when the end section of this was destroyed that a green was created.

Swaffham Bulbeck did not become a port until about 1700, when a single commercial enterprise became established in the separate hamlet of Commercial End, away from the main village. The fine brick Merchant's House dates from this period and later a granary, warehouse, salt house, malting house and several cottages for clerks and workmen were erected. The whole is a good example of the kind of successful but relatively small-scale commercial organisation which was able to flourish before the railway age. As a community, it is unique in the Fenland.

Other villages, both to east and west of Reach and Swaffham Bulbeck, engaged in waterborne commerce and there is evidence that hythes existed at Fen Drayton, Swavesey, Over, Burwell, Soham and Methwold. A fine timber-built warehouse of the fifteenth century survives at Fen Ditton.

Even away from the fen edge, the plan of most Fenland villages is elongated, with the buildings strung out along the village street. Thus the villages lying to the south and west of the Wash have their axes along the road running along the silt ridge (or at least they did before bypasses provided welcome relief from the traffic on the A17 trunk road). The same is true of many villages on islands in the fens: Sibsey, Stickney and Stickford to the north of Boston, Wicken on its peninsula SSE of Ely, Downham and Witchford in the Isle of Ely, and Manea and Coveney which stand on their own islands.

Large villages, like Haddenham or Donington, might have more than one village street, but Fenland villages which are rectangular in plan are quite rare; Heckington, Glinton and Mareham-le-Fen are among the few which qualify.

In most Fenland villages, the manor house is in the village itself and only along the Norfolk fen margin do we find it isolated from the village by an extensive park. This remained true over a long period of history, from the medieval Longthorpe Tower and Northborough Manor right down to the Georgian Frampton Hall and Wyberton Hall. Wilburton exemplifies a later change of taste as here the original manor house (The Burystead) of 1600 is in the village street, whereas its Victorian successor is set well back and screened from the public gaze.

Frampton is a picture-book village. The visitor emerges through the trees to find a medieval church, crowned by one of the earliest broach spires, and the Georgian rectory facing each other across the village street. The Hall (1725) is set back on one side of the rectory and on the other is the Moore's Arms with its ornately carved coat of arms. The village street continues to the east and to the west the view is closed by an eighteenth-century farmhouse at the bend in the road. It is an essentially civilised composition.

Then there are the hamlets on the newlands by the Wash: scattered farmhouses and groups of cottages sheltering behind the sea banks. Surfleet Seas End, although now some miles from the sea, reminds one of the settlements on the Essex marshes—all piles and masts on one side of the bank and the Ship Inn and the cottages on the other.

Gedney Drove End and Dawsmere, on the other hand, turn their backs on the sea and look to the soil for their livelihood. The red brick houses, the dahlias in the cottage gardens and the trees bring colour to the flat landscape. There is an air of prosperity and of tranquillity, the tranquillity that comes from being at the end of a longish road that leads nowhere else.

All these villages have just grown up, new buildings being added as the need arises. Chippenham, however, is a model village, the rural equivalent of the Georgian new towns. The church and the school, facing each other across the village street, form the centre-piece, and on either side are rows of related cottages, some terraced and some semi-detached. At the end of the street are the gates leading to the Park.

Part of Thorney consists of ornate nineteenth-century housing in yellow brick, but the more attractive part of the village is to the south of the abbey church, where the house known as Thorney Abbey (see p 159) faces two elegant stone houses across the green which was formerly the site of the abbey cloister.

The visitor can hardly avoid noticing the large amount of new building in the Fenland villages. The new houses and estates are indistinguishable from those being erected elsewhere in Britain and there is no longer any local style involved. Many older houses, too, are being modernised and attractive dwellings created from barns, stables and other buildings no longer needed for the purpose for which they were built.

The larger villages, particularly those having a scattered plan such as Bottisham and Burwell, can more readily absorb new building and retain their character, whereas a small village like Little Thetford has been utterly overwhelmed by it. It is a question of scale and of sensitivity to the *genius loci*.

8 Domestic Architecture

Building Materials

ALTHOUGH stone was transported by water over quite large distances for the building of abbeys, parish churches, bridges and a few important private dwellings, all other building depended on local materials right up to the nineteenth century.

In medieval times, timber, especially oak, was the most widely used building material. Oak had never been plentiful in the Fens and supplies were becoming scarce in Elizabethan times, though even before then less durable woods were often used for the smaller houses; these included poplar, lime, hornbeam, elm, willow, and alder. The southern boundary of the Fens was, however, an exception and, here, timber-framed buildings continued to be erected right up to the eighteenth century.

When it is considered that, in order to build a two-storey house with a ground floor area of about 600sq ft, it might be necessary to clear fell over an acre of oaks, each of which may have taken a century to mature, it is hardly surprising that timber supplies failed to keep pace with demand.

Other materials were however at hand, the chief of these being brick. The manufacture of bricks seems to have ceased in Britain sometime after the Romans departed, but there are records of bricks being made near Ely in the fourteenth century and during the next hundred years a number of large and important brick buildings were erected in the Fenland; several of these survive and are discussed below.

Where suitable clay was available, the bricks were often made on the actual building site. Nearly all early bricks are red in colour and it was only towards the end of the eighteenth century that the manufacture was intensified of the so-called 'white' bricks which are now so common in the southern Fenland. These owe their rather washed-out yellow colour to the gault clay which was dug from pits at Horningsea, Lode, Stow-cum-Quy and Burwell, to the north-east of Cambridge, and at Haddenham in the Isle of Ely. Since these bricks were hand-made they are not uniform in colour or texture, so that what might otherwise be an overall dullness is relieved by occasional pinks and greys.

Finally, with the invention of the continuously burning Hoffmann Kiln in 1858, the mass production of bricks became possible and was established on the vast bed of Oxford clay at Fletton and Whittlesey. Although Fletton and Whittlesey are in the Fens, the products of their industry have lost all local character and are used throughout Britain in great numbers.

The limestone that was used throughout the Fenland for abbeys and churches was also used for humbler dwellings in the immediate neighbourhood of the quarries. The stone belt centred on Stamford spilt over into the Fens at the Deepings and modest stone buildings are also to be found in Baston and other villages to the north, towards Peterborough in the south and eastwards out into the fen at Crowland. Sometimes only one or two principal faces of a building would be faced with stone or, where all the faces are stone, then perhaps only the front is ashlar with the remainder of rubble masonry.

Elsewhere on the fen margins, building stones of poorer quality were available. Brown carstone, a variety of sandstone, is quarried in north-west Norfolk between Denver and Hunstanton and in the Isle of Ely. In Downham Market and nearby villages, many houses are built of tiny pieces of carstone, coursed as if they were irregular small bricks. Carstone also occurs at the southern end of the Lincolnshire wolds, where the presence of glauconite gives it the greenish tinge characteristic of Spilsby sandstone.

Clunch, the rather soft marly type of chalk formerly quarried at Reach, Burwell and Isleham, was used for building in the southern Fens. A less durable form of chalk-stone occurs in western Norfolk; it is almost identical with the better known Totternhoe stone, quarried near Dunstable and used for many important buildings in the Middle Ages.

Lastly, there is flint. This very hard pure form of silica is found in Norfolk and on the edges of some of the Cambridgeshire fens. Since it only occurs in small pieces, it is invariably used in combination with brick or stone, giving opportunities for making patterns of various kinds.

With ample supplies of reed and sedge available in the undrained fens, thatch was the commonest roof covering throughout the Middle Ages. It was largely displaced by the use of tiles in the eighteenth century, though there are still a good many thatched cottages and houses to be seen in country districts.

Pantiles are more common than plain tiles on older Fenland buildings except in the stone belt where many houses are appropriately roofed with stone slates from the quarries at Collyweston. Materials are however often mixed and one finds stone houses with thatched roofs and many houses of the local redbrick have roofs of grey Welsh slates. All these natural materials go together, particularly when they have weathered, but the same is certainly not true of corrugated sheets of asbestos or steel which have regrettably replaced them on some cottages.

Castles, Country Houses and Rectories

The feudal system under which each peasant owed allegiance to, and was in turn protected by, a great lord hardly existed in the Fens. Most of the peasants were freemen and there were no great secular estates. Consequently few castles were built and their unfortified successors, the large country houses, are equally scarce. Neither the abolition of the monasteries in the sixteenth century, nor the general draining in the seventeenth, seems to have encouraged the new land-owners to abandon their existing residences in order to build vast new mansions in the Fens. Fenland country houses are modest in size and do not attempt to rival, in quantity and sumptiousness, the medieval ecclesiastical architecture throughout the whole area. Which is as it should be.

As part of his plan to govern his newly-won kingdom, William the Conqueror quickly established castles at strategic points, including Cambridge and Wisbech and also along the line of the Roman Ermine Street a few miles beyond the western fen edge. The origin of Ely castle is uncertain: some writers suggest that this was built in 1071 following the suppression of Hereward's rebellion but it is not mentioned in the Domesday book.

These castles were all of the motte and bailey type; that is they comprised a conical mound (the motte) crowned by a keep and a lower outer courtyard (the bailey). At Ely, both motte and bailey survive in the park adjacent to the cathedral; at Cambridge, the motte stands in the grounds of the Shire Hall on Castle Hill. There is nothing to be seen at Wisbech, and at no site does any building survive.

With one splendid exception, very little remains of any of the later castles built around the fen margin: Bolingbroke, Sleaford, Bourne, Woodcroft, Wood Walton, Freckenham and Wormegay. The splendid exception is Castle Rising, the unusually large and decorated keep of which still stands inside a mighty earthwork overlooking the coastal marshes, four miles north-east of King's Lynn.

The earthworks consist of an almost circular enclosure

surrounded by a rampart over 60ft high and a ditch with a scarp going down to 112ft below the top of the ramparts. There are outer enclosures on two sides. The keep, built around 1150, is of the hall type with the hall and the other principal rooms side by side on the first floor and the domestic quarters underneath. The most lavish part of the building is the unusually well-preserved forebuilding with its great staircase leading through three arched doorways to a vaulted vestibule, with two large windows and a decorated Norman doorway leading into the hall. The outer walls are enriched with blank arcading. The whole is a tour-de-force of late Norman military architecture.

At Old Bolingbroke the lower parts of the masonry defences survive, showing that the castle was polygonal in shape with round towers at the angles and a pair forming a gatehouse on the north side. Although Bolingbroke Castle is in the wolds, the castle seems to have relied strongly on water for its protection and so has more in common with the low-lying defensive sites which occur in the northern Fenland at Frampton, Moulton, Swineshead, Wrangle and Wyberton, than with those at Cambridge, Ely or Castle Rising. Such sites are the forerunners of the moated farmhouses of a later period.

An interesting line of partially-built castles can be traced along the southern fen edge; work on these was started by King Stephen in 1144 in order to contain a rebellion by Geoffrey de Mandeville, who had established his base in the Isle of Ely. The best preserved of the sites is at Burwell, but there is evidence of similar ones at Swavesey, Rampton and Cottenham. Work was abandoned following the death of de Mandeville and the collapse of the rebellion.

Longthorpe Tower, near Peterborough, is an early example of a fortified manor house. The tower itself was added to a thirteenth-century house about 1300 and is almost unaltered. It is famous for the almost complete series of fourteenth-century wall paintings in the Great

Chamber on the first floor (see Pl 20, p 173). They were discovered soon after the 1939–45 war and portray a combination of Biblical, moral and secular subjects: a nativity, various apostles, the Seven Ages of Man, the Wheel of the Five Senses and so on. They add up to what the late Professor Saxl described as a 'spiritual encyclopedia' and are all of very high quality.

Longthorpe is the earliest of a number of towers in the Fenland which, while retaining the form of a military building, became more and more domesticated as the centuries passed: South Kyme (stone, mid-fourteenth-century), Tattershall Castle and the Tower-on-the-Moor, the brick gateways at Middleton Towers, Oxburgh Hall and Wiggenhall St Mary Hall (all fifteenth-century), and Rochford and Hussey Towers, near Boston (built of brick c 1510).

Tattershall Castle is one of the most remarkable brick buildings in England. It was begun by Ralph Cromwell, Lord Treasurer of England, in 1434–5 and stands inside a double moat (the outer one is no longer complete). Its vast keep rises 110ft above the level of the flat Fenland and dominates the surrounding countryside (see Pl 23, p 207). The large size of many of the windows and the richly ornamented fireplaces and vaults are ample evidence that the building was intended to be a splendid mansion as well as one capable of defence if need be. The surviving guard-house has been made into a small museum illustrating the history of the site, including that of the stone castle of 1231 which preceded the present keep.

The ornate brick gatehouse of Oxburgh Hall (TF 743013) is one of the earliest and finest of a distinguished group of similar buildings in East Anglia. It was built by Edmund Bedingfeld in 1482 and, although it is now owned by The National Trust, the Hall is still lived in by his descendants—a remarkable record of almost continuous occupation by a single family. Over this period most of the Hall has been considerably altered, but the splendid gatehouse remains as it was built, commanding the bridge across the placid waters of the moat. The quality of the brickwork of the spiral staircase is superb and is hardly rivalled in any other building of the period. Among the furnishings are some panels of needlework by Mary Queen of Scots, worked while she was a prisoner. From the roof, Ely cathedral is visible on a clear day, eighteen miles across the fens, and near at hand the visitor has a birds-eye view of the French parterre garden laid out on the east side of the house about 1830.

The remains of unfortified medieval houses in the Fenland include two country houses built by bishops of Ely and one built by an abbot of Ramsey. These are Biggin Abbey, near Fen Ditton (TL 487617—it was never an abbey), the Bishop's Palace at Downham-in-the-Isle and Bodsey House (TL 295874). Bodsey is the most complete, consisting today of a dwelling dating from the thirteenth century and a chapel added about 100 years later.

Of greater interest is the manor house at Northborough, near Peterborough. It was built in 1330–40 on the traditional plan, still to be found in Cambridge colleges, of a hall on one side of a screens passage, with kitchen, buttery and pantry on the other. Its style is that of the English vernacular and is characterised by its steep triangular gables, mullioned windows and massive chimneys. A separate gateway across the courtyard has independent entrances for carriages and pedestrians. The porch was added to the hall when the house was enlarged and altered early in the seventeenth century.

Cromwell often visited Northborough, for his daughter Elizabeth married one of the Claypoles who owned it, and his widow lived there after his death.

A few miles away at Market Deeping is what is claimed to be the oldest inhabited parsonage house in England. The date of the hall and entrance is thought to be about 1240; the door is the original one and so is the north hall window, with its unusual tracery. The medieval roof beams also survive and carry carved wooden figures of high quality (these are medieval but are later than the beams). The staircase of 1761 is unusual, since it lacks supports and at the same time manages to serve three levels. If the house was indeed a refectory or dormitory used by visiting monks from Croyland Abbey, as is traditionally supposed, that would account for the high quality of the medieval workmanship. Two other Fenland rectories are medieval in origin: Stretham has a fourteenth-century wing and Landbeach a cellar with a vaulted roof of about the same date.

Oxburgh was the fore-runner of a whole series of ornamental brick buildings in East Anglia and of some further afield. In this tradition are the spiral staircases and entrance towers at Upwell Rectory, the decorated east gable at Denver Hall, the north porch at Wallington Hall, the west gable and exotic chimney of the Old Vicarage at Methwold, and the gatehouses to Christ's, St John's and Trinity Colleges, Cambridge.

Apart from the porch, with its terracotta work depicting human and grotesque figures, birds, foliage and emblems, Wallington Hall is of particular interest on account of the carstone and brick chequer-work on the chimney at the east end—a most unusual form of decoration.

From the Tudor period, too, there are survivals of timber-framed manor houses along the southern and eastern fen edges, where oak was still readily obtainable. Burgh Hall at Swaffham Bulbeck and Baldwin Manor at Swaffham Prior are two splendid examples of early sixteenth-century craftmanship. The hipped roof of Baldwin Manor is a feature of Kentish tradition that is rarely found in East Anglian houses of the period, with their prominent gables.

The coming of the Renaissance had little effect on domestic architecture in the Fenland, which is hardly surprising in view of the reluctance with which the new ideas were accepted in Cambridge itself. Houses continued to be built in the English vernacular right up to the seventeenth century. Lovell's Hall, Terrington St Clement (1543), Dowsby Hall (1603–10) and Billingborough Hall (1620) are typical examples. There is little that can be called true Elizabethan now that Beaupré Hall has at last been demolished—in marked contrast to the many great Elizabethan houses elsewhere in England.

At the Reformation the estates of the former abbeys and priories were distributed among the gentry. Some were adapted to meet the needs of their new owners, while the stones of others were used for new buildings either on the site or elsewhere. The process was unhurried. The former Lady Chapel of Ramsey Abbey was adapted in the sixteenth century into an Elizabethan house, though it is hard to tell what this was like as the building history is undocumented and major alterations were made to the house early in the nineteenth century.

The reconstruction of Anglesey Priory (TL 530623) was begun about 1600. Although it incorporates the Monk's Parlour and the Chapter House, the building we see today does in fact owe more to the alterations and additions made in 1861, and even more to those made from 1926 onwards when the house was given new life by Huddleston Broughton, first Lord Fairhaven, who subsequently bequeathed it to The National Trust. The house contains an important collection of paintings, sculpture, books and *objets d'art* and is surrounded by what are, without doubt, the finest gardens in the whole of the Fen country (see p 161).

With the seventeenth century, the number of surviving country houses became greater and much more is known about the architects involved in their design. It seems almost certain, for example, that Dowsby Hall was designed by John Thorpe; the house remains a puzzle, however, since the south front is entirely blank, as if a further part of the house once adjoined it, yet Thorpe's drawings show no evidence of this.

Sometimes we find timber-framed houses being incorporated into later brick buildings. Fen Ditton Hall, for example, which is the eastern half of a large seventeenth-century brick house, has been found to contain part of the timber structure and brick infilling of a fifteenth-century house inside it.

After 1650 we do find major country houses in a style which departs radically from the vernacular of the preceding centuries. Among the earliest are Thorpe Hall, near Peterborough, Thorney Abbey, and the now demolished Wisbech Castle.

Thorpe Hall was built in 1653–6 by Peter Mills, a London architect who was later one of the four men appointed to supervise the rebuilding of the city after the Great Fire. Peter Mills has not been proved to have been associated with the building of Thorney Abbey (1660) or Wisbech Castle (1658) but the similarity of styles suggest that he may well have been. All three were square houses with hipped roofs and large eaves, distinguished though from the mainstream of classical architecture by their unusual details, dubbed by Sir John Summerson 'artisan mannerism'. These are to be seen on the gateposts at Thorpe Hall, the balcony at Wisbech which is now on a house called Castle Lodge, and the doorcases and fireplaces at Thorney. Today Thorney Abbey is the headquarters of a wildlife park and Thorpe Hall has an uncertain future in the ownership of the Greater Peterborough Development Corporation.

Once introduced, artisan mannerism spread throughout the Fenland as builders of lesser houses followed the fashion for adding pediments and other decorative details, often on the slightest excuse and with little regard for their propriety.

The distinguished gentleman-architect, Sir Roger Pratt, retired to his native Norfolk in 1667 and built himself a house at Ryston, near Denver. Ryston Hall was unusual in having only one principal floor, with a basement below and a high hipped roof with dormer windows above it, the whole being capped by a big segmental pediment and a square central pavilion. Subsequent rebuilding by Sir John Soane and by Salvin has left little of Pratt's work.

The industrial revolution hardly affected the Fenland as it lacked all resources of fuel and raw materials. The ports, which served a wider area and through which agricultural produce and coal passed, prospered and the new wealth for building was in the hands of the merchants in the towns rather than of the country landowners. Indeed, the sons of many landowners went into the professions and moved away, abandoning the old halls and manor houses, several of which, particularly near Wisbech, were pulled down in the nineteenth century.

Leverington Hall was one of the survivors in the Wisbech area and its history is typical of such houses elsewhere in the Fens. Originating as an Elizabethan timber-framed house, it seems to have been rebuilt in brick in the second half of the seventeenth century. It was modernised internally in 1716 and its outward appearance given a fashionable facelift.

Among the few notable Georgian country houses in the Fens are Frampton Hall and Wyberton Hall. Frampton Hall is the earliest and is noted especially for its 'gorgeous rainwater heads, among the finest in England', as Pevsner describes them. Wyberton Hall was built in 1761 and may well have been the work of the younger William Sands. It contains some fine wood panelling and plaster ceilings.

Notwithstanding the fact that Capability Brown settled at Fenstanton, nowhere in the Fenland is there any landscaped park by him or in the style which he helped to create.

Of Victorian country houses, there is little to be said.

Revesby Abbey by William Burn combines continental themes of more than one period with a baroque interior. Pugin's Wilburton Manor, on the other hand, is restrained in style and harps back to the English vernacular, but is utterly asymmetric.

The greatest contribution of the twentieth century is not a house but a garden—the garden of Anglesey Abbey, created by Lord Fairhaven from 1926 onwards. The site has no natural features apart from the quarry from which coprolite had once been extracted—otherwise it is entirely level. Here then, within an area of 90 acres, is a series of intimate gardens surrounded by larger areas in which free landscape is contrasted with formal avenues on a scale and with a grandeur reminiscent of the eighteenth century, everywhere enhanced by well-sited urns, statuary and temples. It is a remarkable creation which has not yet reached its full maturity.

Village Architecture

From the manor house and the grander kind of parsonage house, we move on to consider the humbler dwellings which make up the bulk of any village: the smaller farmhouses, the cottages, the shops and the pubs.

To study their building history, the lack of written records makes it necessary to adopt the methods of the archaeologist rather than the historian. Fortunately many buildings have survived from earlier periods which can be examined and measured; the occurrence of particular features can then be mapped and statistical procedures used to build up a general picture.

Most Fenland villages contain one or more houses dating from the sixteenth or seventeenth century, which escaped the extensive rebuilding that seems to have occurred in the period between 1770 and 1870. Most surviving sixteenth-century village houses and farmhouses have timber frames; originally the walls would have been panelled with a mixture of mud and straw or some similar material, and the roof thatched. After 1600 however, brick, which had hitherto been regarded as a luxury reserved for grander houses, began to be used more widely. The two reasons for this were the scarcity of timber throughout the Fenland and the influence of the Dutch, which showed itself in ways discussed below.

The surviving timber-framed house may still be panelled with mud, but equally well the mud is likely to have been replaced by chalk or by brick nogging. We can rarely tell from the outside because so often the whole exterior has been plastered over to keep out the weather. More significant therefore is the presence of an overhanging upper storey. Some timber-framed houses have even been completely encased in brick, their original mode of construction only coming to light during alterations. During Queen Elizabeth's reign, the chimney stack which had formerly been on the outside of buildings was moved towards the centre where it was able to serve more than one room. Later when the upper part of the house began to be used for living accommodation rather than solely for storage, the same chimney stack could be made to serve the rooms there.

The bricks used during the seventeenth and eighteenth centuries were dark red in colour, often with a bluish tinge, were irregular in shape and surface texture, and were somewhat thinner than the modern machine-made bricks. The houses were characterised by their gabled ends, which were steeper than on most modern houses and were often tumbled—that is they incorporated triangular wedges of bricks set at right angles to the line of the gable.

At about the same time that brick began to be used for smaller buildings, pantiles began to replace thatch for roofing. Now, pantiles are hung on to the laths without nailing, so it is essential to prevent wind from getting under a pantiled roof and lifting it. This was achieved in Fenland houses by carrying the gable up above the level of the roof. It is unnecessary to do this with thatched roofs, both because these are tied down to the rafters and because, being permeable, dangerously high pressure differences cannot build up across the roof to dislodge it. Most thatched roofs do therefore have substantial eaves.

Tumbled gables and the introduction of pantiles are two examples of the Dutch influence. Others are the occasional use of ornamental gables incorporating curves—Dutch gables first appear in Cambridge in the 1630s—and the change in arrangement of the bricks which occurred in the second half of the seventeenth century when Flemish bond (with headers and stretchers alternating in each course of brickwork) replaced English bond (alternate courses of headers and stretchers). For a time, too, Dutch bricks and tiles were imported through the Wash ports to supplement local supplies.

In those parts of the Fens adjacent to the limestone belt, timber was again the normal structural material for smaller dwellings so long as adequate supplies remained available. However, the demand for housing after the Civil War and the destruction of timber resources during it, forced builders to make much greater use of stone and many stone houses therefore date from the period 1660–1720.

Gables that are carried up above the roof line are also a feature of those stone houses whether they be roofed with pantiles, stone slates or even thatch. Bay windows were another feature which became popular in stone houses at this time, though the fashion was stronger in towns than in the countryside.

Neither carstone nor chalk was used for house building before the eighteenth century. Soon after that, white bricks became fashionable, so that there was then a wide range of materials available in the Fenland which could be juxtaposed to give various kinds of wall patterns and to emphasise doors, windows and quoins.

Thus flint and brick are used together along the Norfolk fen edge and also in some of the villages further south (eg Horningsea). Carstone and brick occur together again in Norfolk, and at Horbling we find brick quoins used on limestone walls. The use of red bricks to emphasise features on a building predominantly of white brick was widespread, and a particular feature of the many non-conformist chapels which sprang up in the nineteenth century

Artisan mannerism, which we noted on larger buildings (p 159), is also to be seen on smaller seventeenth-century houses and pubs where it takes the form of strange and uncoordinated details, such as the brick quoins, string courses and pediments on the King's Head at Kirton-in-Holland, the Red Lion at Bicker and Porch House at Sibsey. (Church House at Boston is another example.) With these stylistic exceptions, Fenland village architecture is essentially practical, but one example of the picturesque is worth mentioning: the Round House at Little Thetford (TL 532763), a circular red-brick cottage with a thatched roof modelled on the South African *Rondavel* and probably built in the eighteenth century.

After about 1700, the need for increased sleeping accommodation in farmhouses and cottages led to the introduction of dormer windows in the roof and the installation of permanent staircases. The roofs of many Fenland dormers are carried back to the ridge line in a single slope, thus avoiding many of the difficulties which would otherwise arise from the use of pantiles.

Later in the eighteenth century, the mansard roof was introduced from Holland and became a feature of many village houses in East Anglia and the southern Fens. This form of pitched roof had two slopes on either side, the lower being steeper than the upper, thus greatly increasing the amount of space inside the roof. Haddenham has a particularly good collection of cottages with mansard roofs.

In the nineteenth century, white brick established itself as the predominant building material in the southern Fens, with Welsh slates as the main roofing material. Red brick and pantiles continued to hold their own in the Lincolnshire Fens and were used for many of the smallholders' cottages built at that time; roofs were, however, less steep, gables no longer rose above the roof line, and chimneys were once again at the ends of buildings.

So far we have not mentioned almhouses or village schools. The most attractive almhouses are those forming the Howard Hospital at Castle Rising; this quadrangle of single-storeyed houses with a projecting chapel was built in 1614 and retains its original Jacobean furniture. At Tattershall, there is a much plainer range of seventeenth-century almhouses near the church, and behind one of the houses on the south side of the square are the remains of the medieval school.

The village school at Chippenham (see p 148) is unusual in its date (1714) and is a stately red brick building, a change from the usual nineteenth-century Gothic, of which Sir Gilbert Scott's Algakirk is a particularly good example. One cannot leave schools without mentioning Impington Village College, the only building in England with which Walter Gropius was associated, regarded by Sir Nikolaus Pevsner as 'one of the best buildings of its date [1938] in England, if not the best' and the inspiration for many subsequent schools.

From schools to lock-ups—there are good examples at Fenstanton (brick with a clock on top, probably seventeenth century) and at Deeping St James, where a former fifteenth-century market cross was converted into a lock-up in 1819.

9   Engineering Works—
old and new

Windpumps and Windmills

W E have seen in Chapter 3 how it was that wind-powered drainage mills were introduced into the Fens in order to lift the water from the sinking peatlands into the main drains and rivers. There is a record of a mill at work at Holbeach in 1588, though it is known that they had been in use in the Netherlands over 150 years earlier.

Mr Rex Wailes has estimated that before the coming of steam power there were over 2,000 drainage windmills in the Fenland. Of these, only the small mill at Wicken Fen now survives in working order, though a medium sized mill, rather more typical of the breed, is preserved on Herringfleet marshes, in north-east Suffolk.

Fenland drainage mills were almost all smock mills; that is, they had tapering wooden towers, often octagonal in plan, but sometimes having four, six, ten or twelve sides. They rarely had fantails but were turned manually by means of a tailpole, in the Dutch manner. The last large mill of this kind was at Soham Mere—it was built in 1867 and demolished in 1948. Its sails had a span of 80ft and they drove a scoop wheel 28ft 6in in diameter with paddles 12in wide. Such a mill was capable of draining 500–600 acres of land and could lift water through a height equal to about one-fifth the diameter of the scoop wheel.

The small mill at Wicken Fen was originally on

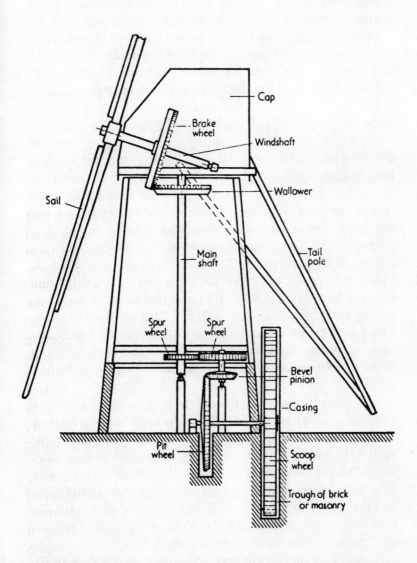

Labels in figure:
- Cap
- Brake wheel
- Windshaft
- Wallower
- Sail
- Tail pole
- Main shaft
- Spur wheel
- Spur wheel
- Bevel pinion
- Casing
- Pit wheel
- Scoop wheel
- Trough of brick or masonry

Fig 3 General arrangement of a large drainage mill. In smaller mills, the bevel pinion was often mounted on the mainshaft and drove the pit wheel directly instead of through a pair of spur wheels

Adventurer's Fen, where it drained a holding of 30 acres. It was built in 1908 as a skeleton mill and the weatherboarding added two years later. It is square in section and has a direct drive from the main shaft to the scoop wheel, which is therefore centrally placed in the tower, with its casing projecting at either end.

On the Norfolk Broads, where most of the later mills were brick-built tower mills and the drainage problems were much less severe, a number of mills have survived and are now preserved. It is a matter for the deepest regret that no large Fenland drainage mill has been preserved in the same way and the enthusiast must content himself with searching out the scanty remains of the buildings of four mills and with tracing the sites of others from the arrangements of the drains and the presence of reservoirs. The four mills are Middle Mill, Mildenhall Fen (TL 631786), Lotting Fen Mill near Ramsey St Mary's (TL 249876) and two mills at Nordelph which operated a double lift (TF 561009 and 561004). The Lotting Fen Mill, built in 1872, was of particular interest in that an auxiliary steam engine was provided to drive the scoopwheel when there was insufficient wind.

The development of the corn mill continued in the Fenland for some years after drainage windmills had been largely replaced by steam engines, and culminated in the building of the multi-sailed tower mills which were among the most sophisticated mills in England. One of the last to be built was the six-sailed Trader Mill at Sibsey in Lincolnshire. Its brick tower of about 75ft high supports an ogee-shaped cap, 16ft in diameter and 10ft high; all the moving parts are of iron.

Another preserved seven-storey mill is the five-sailed Maud Foster mill at Boston. An even larger tower still stands at Moulton; it retains its machinery and is in use as a corn store, though the sails were taken off 80 years ago. There were a few eight-sailed mills in the Fenland and of these only the one at Heckington still carries its

168

sails. Among other preserved corn mills are Downfield
Mill at Soham and Denver Mill; Downfield Mill is
unusual in having once been a wooden smock mill which
was severely damaged in a gale and then rebuilt in
brick with an octagonal base and a round tower.

Watermills

In the fens themselves, with their slow-moving rivers
and virtual absence of fall, watermills can never have
flourished, though we know that some existed. Round
the edge of the fens, however, particularly adjacent to
the great corn-growing region of East Anglia, there
were many mills. Some of these were sited on the main
rivers and their tributaries and others on smaller
streams which have virtually dried up today.

None of the mills is today using water power to grind
corn but some, such as those at Swaffham Bulbeck,
Soham and Mildenhall, are still corn mills. Mills also
survive at Cambridge, Quy, Lode and Bottisham, at
Northwold and Hilborough on the Wissey, and at
Narborough on the Nar. The best preserved of these
eastern mills is probably the one at Lode, which forms
part of the Anglesey Abbey estate (pl 10, p 87). This
timber mill of three floors bears the date 1868 but may
well be older. It contains four pairs of stones driven by
a comparatively wide breast shot wheel. Such wide
wheels are typical of mills in eastern England, since
they derived maximum power from comparatively slow-
moving rivers.

Along the western edge of the fens there are surviving
mills on the main rivers but hardly any elsewhere. The
great timber mill at Houghton on the Ouse, now a Youth
Hostel, is well known and there are also mills at St Ives,
at Water Newton on the Nene, and at Market Deeping
and West Deeping on the Welland.

Where mills no longer exist there are often street
names or other indications that they once did. There is

plenty of scope for amateur detective work in tracing the sites of such mills.

Steam Pumping Engines

The circumstances surrounding the introduction of steam pumping engines to the work of fen drainage have already been described (p 49). Here we are concerned with the engines themselves and with the equipment they drove to raise the water from the main drains into the rivers.

The archetypal fen drainage engine was a single-cylinder double-acting low-pressure condensing beam engine driving a scoopwheel of the pattern used on the windpumps which the steam engines replaced. These

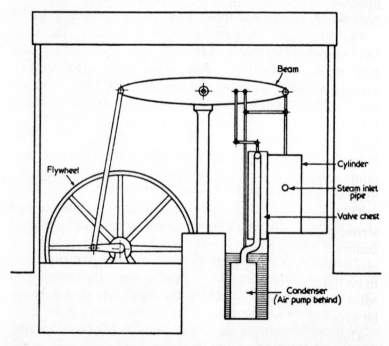

Fig 4 General arrangement of a typical beam engine. The flywheel shaft drove a pinion wheel inside the scoopwheel which was in a separate section of the building

monuments to nineteenth-century engineering skill were so massively built that many of them had a working life of over 100 years. Consequently, there were few opportunities for replacing them with more modern types of steam engine and the lifespan of a single engine often stretched from the windmill age right down to the era of the diesel or electric pump.

It is fortunate that a typical member of the breed has been preserved at Stretham, on the Old West River, south of Ely (TL 516730), and can be seen by the public. Like all the larger engines, it is housed in a tripartite building, with the engine house in the centre, the boilers in a much lower building on one side and the scoop-wheel on the other. Smaller engines, on the other hand, such as the surviving engines at Pinchbeck Marsh, near Spalding (TF 262262), and Dogdyke, near Tattershall (TF 206558), fitted comfortably into a single building.

The Pinchbeck Marsh engine which operated from 1833 to 1952, had a nominal output of 20hp and drove a 22ft diameter scoopwheel with 40 ladles to drain an area of 4,000 acres. It will form the nucleus of a small museum being established by the Welland and Deepings Internal Drainage Board, which is also to contain a 1920 Ruston oil engine from Kirton and Frampton Marsh Pumping Station and a Holmes turbine pump with apple-wood gears installed in 1887 at North Fen Pumping Station, Northborough.

The great weight of the larger engines necessitated strong foundations; at Stretham there was a bed of hard concrete gravel beneath the peat on which to build, but elsewhere several hundred piles and cross timbers had to be driven into the clay to make a firm support for the solid blocks of masonry on which the engine itself was to be erected.

The scoopwheels, too, were very heavy in large engines. They had cast iron centres and all except the earliest incorporated an internal gear wheel driven by a pinion on the main engine shaft. The projecting wooden boards (ladles) rotated in a trough of stone or masonry, with as little clearance as possible to reduce leakage round the edges. The 50ft diameter wheel on the Hundred Foot engine—the largest in the Fens—weighed 75 tonnes.

The Stretham engine had three boilers, others only one or two: two smaller ones were usually more economical than a single large one and a third provided a spare. The early boilers had their fires underneath, but these were later replaced by types having furnaces in tubes inside them. Such a change raised the working pressure of the Stretham engine from 4lb to 8lb per sq in and increased its power output from 60hp to 90hp; the power was also increased by installing new valves. Such improvements were common during the working lives of the engines and enabled them to cope more effectively with the greater loads imposed on them as the surface of the peat fell. Also, it was often necessary to increase the diameter of the scoopwheels so that they could reach down further into the drains.

Not all the engines were beam engines driving scoop-wheels, though this was by far the commonest type. The Waldersea engine (TF 433063) was a Cornish-type engine driving a bucket pump, but it was not a success. Elsewhere side-lever marine-type engines were installed and there were some grasshopper engines; these were preferred where the foundations were really poor as they were lighter than the beam engines.

After 1851, Appold centrifugal pumps became more popular and were used instead of scoopwheels in new installations, as for example at Hobhole Sluice, where the two Appold pumps were driven by high-pressure condensing vertical-cylinder steam engines. The final development of the steam pump in the Fens was the 400hp marine engine and Gwynne centrifugal pump which replaced the Hundred Foot engine in 1914.

Yet another type of steam pumping engine may be seen at the Cambridge Museum of Technology, which

Plate 20 Fourteenth-century paintings on the north wall of the Great Chamber at Longthorpe Tower, showing a nativity scene and the seven ages of man. The paintings at Longthorpe constitute the most complete scheme of domestic mural decoration of the period in England (*Crown Copyright Reserved*)

Plate 21 (above) Harvesting dwarf beans for freezing (A. F. Kersting)

Plate 22 (below) Rows of celery contribute to the pattern of an autumn landscape. The line of a roddon can be seen crossing the celery field (K. A. Hitch)

occupies the site of the former Cheddars Lane pumping station, built in 1895 to pump sewage, previously discharged direct into the river Cam, to a sewage farm at Milton. The two Hathorn–Davey Tandem Compound engines preserved there are thought to be the only surviving examples of engines fitted with Davey differential valve gear, which automatically regulated the supply of steam to correspond to the load on the pumps.

Sluices and Other Drainage Works

The percipient visitor to the Fenland will soon recognise that sluice gates are of many different kinds, each being adapted to the particular task for which it was installed and embodying the technology of the period at which it was built.

The Grand Sluice at Boston, for example, is still very much as it was when it was built in 1766, with masonry walls and abutments and hand-operated wooden doors. The original lock was widened and deepened in 1884 and five out of the six sets of doors were renewed between 1937 and 1956; the age of the other set—the centre set of sea doors—is not known.

The North Level Sluice on the river Nene below Wisbech (and just above the site of the earlier Gunthorpe Sluice) was built nearly a century later under the direction of George Stephenson. Cast iron now makes its appearance, particularly in the footbridge added a few years afterwards to form a strut to give stability to the wing walls. Semicircular sections of a caisson are kept on the site for use when repairs have to be made, but they have been needed only three times since 1859.

At Denver the abutments of Sir John Rennie's sluice of 1832 still remain, although modern lifting steel gates have been installed and the sluice has been widened. The gates here are of a type which is now very common throughout the Fenland, trusses on the back of the gates providing the rigidity and strength to resist the enormous pressures which build up in time of flood. Sometimes two sets of gates face in opposite directions, as they do at Dog-in-a-Doublet Sluice, so as to be able to resist pressure either from floodwater coming downstream or from tidal surges coming up.

With the building of the Relief Channel and the Cut-off Channel, there is now a whole complex of sluices at Denver (Pl 7, p 85). The entrance to the Relief Channel is controlled by the Head Sluice and there is an Impounding Sluice across the Cut-off Channel. A channel above the Impounding Sluice leads to the Diversion Sluice on the Ely Ouse and is the route by which water is diverted into the Cut-off Channel for pumping to the Essex rivers. A channel to the Ely Ouse below the Impounding Sluice is controlled by the Residual Flow Sluice.

The sluices at the seaward ends of the Great Ouse Relief Channel and the Coronation Channel on the Welland have horizontally pivoted flap gates; these open automatically when the water in the channel is above that on the tidal side and close again as the tide rises.

Less obtrusive types of horizontally-pivoted gates may be adequate in some situations. Two types are the electrically-controlled radial gates at Earith which admit water to the Old Bedford River in times of flood and the so-called 'fish-belly' gates which are almost wholly underwater; the Diversion Sluice at Denver is of this type as are many of the sluices in the upper reaches of the river Ouse.

The need to keep the internal drainage systems separate from the high-level rivers has made it necessary to install siphons to carry one under the other and near Outwell there is a small aquaduct where the Well Creek is carried over the Middle Level Main Drain.

Railways and Docks

The construction of railways on peat presents peculiar problems, particularly where the peat is undrained, as it was in Holme Fen when the Great Northern Railway was built across it in 1850. Here the engineer Stephen Ballard used alternate layers of faggots and peat sods to build the base on which the causeway was erected, something like seven times the usual amount of material being required to raise an embankment four feet above the level of the fen.

In the drained area of the Fenland, railway tracks tend to sink an average of ½–1in each year, though this may be rather more in an abnormally dry summer. The sinking is not uniform since the railways cross islands and roddons, and bridges and culverts are built on piles reaching down into the underlying clay. Consequently, constant maintenance is needed to ease gradients and to reconstruct culverts in order to keep them functioning at the right level.

As elsewhere in Britain, the network of local lines has been reduced to a few through routes on which all but the more important stations have been closed. Wisbech no longer has any passenger service and Boston can only be reached by a roundabout route through Sleaford. On the other hand, for the long distance traveller, connections with main lines outside the Fenland have greatly improved. Although it is certainly optimistic to regard the reopening, in 1975, of the formerly-closed stations at Magdalen Road, between Downham Market and King's Lynn, and Ruskington and Metheringham, between Sleaford and Lincoln, as heralding a revival of railways in the area, it at least marks a welcome change from the previous policy.

One of the most interesting casualties was the Wisbech and Upwell Tramway opened in 1883–4 as an experimental 'feeder' light railway by the Great Eastern Railway Company. For most of its route from Wisbech to Outwell, it followed the public road so that the tram engines had their motion encased and were fitted with cow catchers. Notwithstanding the fact that the line was standard gauge, a speed limit of 8 mph was laid down.

177

Competition from motor buses killed the passenger traffic in 1928 but the line continued to carry fruit and other agricultural produce until 1966. The body of one of the original Wisbech and Upwell Tramway coaches, similar to that used in the film *Titfield Thunderbolt*, has been recovered by members of the Cambridge Society for Industrial Archaeology and is now at the Cambridge Museum of Technology.

Another much regretted closure was that of the Midland and Great Northern Joint Railway, whose connections with its parent companies ran across the Fens from Bourne and from Peterborough to a junction at Sutton Bridge, whence it continued eastwards to King's Lynn and the Norfolk coast. Few companies have inspired such loyalty in its employees and regular travellers; its passing was mourned by all who lived within reach of it.

Just north of Sutton Bridge are the derelict wooden wharves and training walls of the entrance to a tidal basin, now occupied by a golf course: the remains of an ill-fated scheme to establish a new port there in 1881. A few days after it had been opened, it was found that the whole construction stood on treacherous sand and part of it collapsed shortly after. Although powers were taken to reopen it in 1895, the basin was never rebuilt.

10 Fenland Agriculture

Introduction

THE physical factors that influence the agriculture of any region are its topography, soils and climate: in the Fens these combine to produce conditions ideally suited to intensive crop production. Coupled with the traditional expertise in arable and horticultural farming that has been built up over the years, it can be understood how the Fens have become the most intensively cultivated and most productive area in Great Britain.

The flat rectangular topography, with many of the field edges along relatively recently dug waterways, cut in straight lines, and with even the roads taking sudden right-angled turns, makes the fields simple to work, flat and square cut. The only curve visible in the whole landscape is often a roddon or an old hedge set on a parish boundary at the base of a fen island.

Many locals would agree with the old adage that the Fens have no climate, just a succession of weather: certainly a winter's day spent riddling out potatoes on the black fen, or by the Marshland coast, would be a daunting experience for most townsmen. The prevailing winds come from south and west, with an incidence of almost 40 per cent throughout the year from that quarter. Only in the early spring do the cold north or north-east winds blow in from the North Sea with any frequency. Rainfall amounts are very small; the area from Cambridge to the Wash is the driest in

Britain with a mean annual total of around 560mm (22 in) which, except for a tendency to a slightly drier period in spring, is spread evenly over the twelve months.

The lack of rainfall leaves many crops short of water during the growing season so irrigation is becoming increasingly important in the raising of high value crops such as celery. Similarly, the growing of grass is difficult; this crop will not grow freely when the soil moisture deficit (the amount by which the potential transpiration exceeds the rainfall) is greater than 50mm (2in). This condition occurs on average on nearly 60 days in each growing season of fewer than 200 days in the Fens.

Temperatures govern the growing season, which begins when the mean air temperature reaches 5°C (41°F) in spring and ends when it falls to the same level in autumn. Coastal regions, with a slightly smaller range in temperature than those further inland, thus have a longer growing season, though this advantage is small, especially as the black peat soils warm up very quickly in the spring. More sunshine is recorded on the coast, though it suffers from sea mists and overcast conditions during summer easterlies and the more humid conditions are often reflected in the incidence of fungus diseases such as septoria on wheat, and potato blight.

Winds are of great importance to the fen farmer and, because of the open nature of the area, some form of windbreak or shelter is often desirable for the more valuable horticultural crops. On the coast, cold easterlies can damage early crops and, in dry conditions in spring time, young crops of all types growing on peat are at constant risk from blowing top soil. Fen blows occur on average about three times in every year, although actual gale force winds are experienced inland rather less frequently.

On the whole it can be seen that the Fen climate, although not producing very early crops, is suited to intensive arable and horticultural farming rather than for grassland husbandry. In the absence of any major differences in climate and topography, it is to the soils that we look in order to understand variations in farming patterns over the Fenland.

In England and Wales, all soils have recently been subjected to a classification survey by the Land Service of the Ministry of Agriculture's Advisory and Development Service; they have been mapped out to show five different grades of soil, according to particular physical capabilities for agricultural use. Grade 1 land is classified as having very minor or no physical limitations to agricultural use, showing high yields and flexible cropping; Grade 2 land has only minor limitations in its range of horticultural and perhaps root crops. The classification continues to Grade 5 land which is generally only suitable for grass or rough grazing.

The Eastern region of England has more Grade 1 and 2 agricultural land (11 per cent and 33 per cent respectively) than any other region in England and Wales. This is due in large part to the Fenlands, where most of the black peatlands are classified Grade 1 and the siltlands Grade 2, the two together forming an enormous acreage of the very best agricultural soils.

Fenland agriculture is based on the 'golden tripod' of potatoes, wheat and sugar-beet, the three crops being grown throughout the region. With this basic rotation a very wide range of vegetable crops, grown on a large, field scale, is interwoven with the agricultural crops proper and this is where the silts tend to differ from the peatlands. Peas and beans are found on both soils, as are onions, though the latter crop is concentrated on the black soils. Cauliflowers, sprouts and cabbages, which need a firm soil, are siltland crops, whereas root crops such as carrots and celery need to be easily washed and so are found on the light peat soils rather than on the stickier silts. Bulbs are almost exclusively a silt crop, as are the best strawberries, but both these high value crops are now also seen on the more mineralised peat areas. Top and soft fruit, too, need the stronger rooting medium offered by the silt.

The Fenland, then, is a region rich in agricultural tradition and expertise and is equally well endowed with raw material and physical climate, where modern intensive cropping systems can be seen at their best.

History of Agriculture in the Fens

After the Roman withdrawal, when the fens had once again become wet and untenable, only the barest subsistence agriculture would have been possible except on the drier parts of the silt fens where some of the land would be winterground, that is land that could be cultivated or used by stock over winter. Elsewhere, and especially on the peat, there was only summerground available, with coarse grazing and some hay making during the drier months.

The fens were remote, unhealthy and dangerous; the Fenmen an independent breed of tough cottagers and squatters, living in cabins on the higher ground, plying across the marshes on stilts and jumping poles, grazing their stock, fishing and fowling. The more populous area to the north was dotted with mixed farms of enclosed corn and grass fields, with many shared common grazing lands. The fens were noted for their fine sheep, either 'Norfolks' or 'Lincolns', which had the longest carcase and legs of any British breed; they were heavily fleeced, fattened beautifully and were impervious to wet ground. Winter beef and mutton fattened well on arable plots of mustard and cole-seed and the breeding of shire horses was well established, the young stock being sent to the Midlands for breaking in.

Following the drainage in the seventeenth century, the peat fens began to come into the agricultural picture; at first, there was so much organic material in the soil that much of the top layer was pared off and burnt. Among the first crops sown were hemp, flax, woad, mustard and cole-seed (what we now know as rape). Cole-seed was a marvellous crop, fields being sown in succession to fold sheep, for which it acted as a superb fattener throughout the winter months. Then in spring it was left to run to seed and sold for its oil content. In summer, there was plenty of grazing available, so stock could be kept in good condition all the year round. With improved drainage and better conditions on the land, brood mares and their offspring could now be used for draught, where beforehand the wet land would only bear the weight of small ponies. In this way farming became more mechanised and efficient, with more land coming under the management of the bigger farmers. The old breed of fen slodgers were now reduced to working for the wealthy landowners and the fens became properly populated for the first time.

During this period—the beginning of the eighteenth century—the fen sheep were crossed selectively with Midland breeds to improve the general stock, and on the arable side the potato appeared and was very soon established as an important Fenland crop. By mid-century the beginning of the agricultural revolution was in sight: throughout the country an increasing population demanded more food production, and enclosure acts were hastened by the spread of disease among common-land herds and by disputes between commoners over the unfair distribution of rights. Much of the grazing land began to be turned over to the plough; whole landscapes were transformed, as well as the lives of the people. Where they had been shepherds, reared geese, fished and fowled, they now became farm labourers and ploughmen on corn land.

One of the more notorious episodes in the history of Fenland agriculture was the riot of 1816 which began in Littleport and spread into Ely. As a direct result of the long war against France, culminating at Waterloo in

FENLAND AGRICULTURE

1815, economic distress was rife, and as is so often the case, poor people, including the agricultural labourers, were among the worst affected. Even an Act of Parliament passed to give aid to the poor increased their distress, for if a labourer could receive a supplementary grant to maintain his family, then why should the farmer pay anything but a minimum wage?

After the war, wages fell steadily and the price of corn was halved, despite a succession of poor harvests. Then, with a labourer's wage held at 9s a week, corn doubled in price over a single season and food prices rocketed. Disturbances occurred all over the country, machines were smashed in the North and Midlands and a mob attempted to take the Tower of London. Even in East Anglia, the usually phlegmatic labourers banded together and talked riot and destruction. Uprisings in Norfolk spread through Downham Market, reaching the ears of the Littleport men. At one of the weekly meetings of the benefit club, a semi-political speaker was expected from across the border at Southery. He did not appear, and soon a number of the men, in a rather ugly mood, no doubt, went out to meet him. By accident or design, a stone was thrown, a window broken and goods seized from inside. Despite a plea from the vicar, the mob tore through the village, smashing more windows and looting food and spirits. Arguments and fighting increased the confusion; the vicar's own house was broken into and he fled to warn the magistrates at Ely, 5 miles down the road.

East Anglia's own Paul Revere, Mr Archer—a member of the well known Ely legal family—was despatched with all haste to get help from the militia at Bury. While he galloped the 30 miles into the garrison town and returned with a small platoon of Royal Dragoons, the rioters armed themselves with pitchforks, set up a fowling-piece on a farm cart and marched into Ely. In the market place they were addressed from the high windows of the White Hart by Mr Metcalf, the magis-

184

trate, but he could not calm them, so undeterred, the mob smashed and looted their way down Fore Hill and Broad Street, where they were warned of the arrival of troops and set off hurriedly for home in stolen carts.

The Dragoons, reinforced by local militia from Ely, marched off in pursuit, charged down Littleport main street and finally cornered the rioters in the George and Dragon. A sharp volley through the windows soon brought out the mob for a final skirmish and most of the men were soon arrested. One, called Sindall, broke away from his guards and was shot dead as he attempted to escape. Altogether 75 persons were apprehended, and amounts of stolen property and cash recovered. Other members of the riotous mob scattered into the fens, with a reward of £5 on each head.

In June 1816, 51 people were eventually brought to stand trial in Ely for rioting and disturbing the peace. The court sat for a week hearing many charges of damaging property and stealing goods or money, though a great number of the defendants had no clear ideas as to why the offences had been committed.

Five men were condemned to hang, five sentenced to transportation for life and eleven (including one woman) to one year's confinement in prison; all the rest were discharged. On Friday, 28 June, Will Beamiss, George Crow, John Dennis, Isaac Harley and Thomas Smith made the journey by black-draped cart from Market Street to the scaffold in Mill Pits. Their bodies were buried together in St Mary's Churchyard under the inscription 'May their awful fate be a warning to others'.

In the thirty years following the Napoleonic wars, methods of farming changed radically for the better, particularly in south Lincolnshire, and crop yields were almost doubled. Mixed farming took the place of pasture and farmers concentrated on growing a narrower range of crops. Prices, for wheat in particular, remained low and it was only by improving their standard of

FENLAND AGRICULTURE

husbandry, employing less labour and increasing crop yields, that Fenland farmers on the heavier soils of Lincolnshire could remain solvent.

About the same time, the introduction of machinery began to make a major impact on Fenland farming. Threshing machines were a common sight by the 1840s and McCormick's reaper was imported from America soon after. Several manufacturers established themselves in or near the Fenland: Richard Hornsby at Grantham, Tuxford and Sons at Boston, and Clayton and Shuttleworth at Lincoln. Another such firm was founded by Frederick Savage at King's Lynn in 1853. Within a few years, Frederick Savage was not only manufacturing ploughing, winding, traction and portable engines, as well as all kinds of agricultural implements, but was also making substantial contributions to their development and was winning awards for reliability and ingenuity at agricultural shows throughout eastern England. Later Mr Savage's genius was directed to the manufacture and development of steam-driven fairground machinery, including 'gallopers', 'razzle dazzles', 'steam yachts', 'gondola switchbacks' and other equipment with equally exotic but now largely forgotten names.

The later nineteenth century was once again marked by an agricultural depression, but this was weathered rather better in the Fens than elsewhere, the multitude of smallholdings of around ten acres being quite sufficient to support a family. The Fenmen did not have to rely on corn and beef for their living; vegetables, fruit, turnips, carrots and celery paid handsomely and were grown with great success. During the depression, the Fens followed the countrywide pattern of diminishing corn acreage, with 20 per cent less grown in the last decade of the century. However, the potato acreage increased rapidly; in 1900 alone, the acreage under potatoes in Lincolnshire jumped by 10 per cent to 64,000. At that time the average yield per acre of

186

potatoes over the whole country was under 6 tons, of wheat 15cwt, and barley 17cwt. Corn was worth 26s a quarter and cattle less than £2 per live cwt.

Cereal crops were all cut and stacked for threshing later; harvest began in early August and often did not finish for up to eight weeks. In a good season, for example 1910, the harvest began in East Anglia on 14 August and was finished by 19 September.

A most important event for the Fenland was the introduction of sugar-beet in the 1920s. In 1924, there were three beet sugar factories in the Fens and a subsidy was given for growing the crop. The popularity of sugar-beet increased rapidly, for it grew well and gave a good profit, besides fitting in very well with the Fenland cropping programme. By 1930, the price was 49s per ton, and the acreage was increasing by up to 50 per cent every year.

Mechanisation of farms began: in 1890 over 1,000,000 horses were working in the Isle of Ely and Lincolnshire but by 1930 they had dwindled to a quarter of that figure. The era of modern agricultural practice had begun; the 1930 average yields of wheat—17 cwt per acre, and potatoes—6½ tons per acre, which had been more or less static for many years were to double in the next two decades, as the tilling of the land grew up into a modern business.

Fruit and Vegetables

Since horticulture plays such a big part in modern Fenland life, it is worth taking a separate look at the history of its development. Horticulture is really a modern development of agriculture; its success depends upon the quick distribution of fresh produce to centres of population or upon facilities for drying, canning, or freezing such produce—all of which have been available only in relatively recent times. It is thought that fruit growing in the Fens began as far back as Roman times, with the introduction of the apple orchard, but the next indication of anything other than backyard production was the practice of Flemish immigrants during the sixteenth and seventeenth centuries, who grew onions and sold them in quantity at Peterborough and Stourbridge fairs.

It was the arrival of the railways that made large-scale fruit and vegetable growing an economic possibility in the Fens; previously there had been only a few old cider orchards and small growers of vegetable crops for local markets.

The most famous fruit growing family was Chivers of Histon, a name that is still known throughout Britain, although take-over bids have obscured the original connections. In 1850, Stephen Chivers and his son John had three acres of fruit at Histon, supplying local markets; by 1860 they were running 160 acres of top and soft fruits, and in 1873 opened a jam factory in the village. By the end of the century, they controlled the produce of 3,000 acres in the surrounding villages, and in 1894 had been the first people to preserve fruit in cans.

The growers originated their own varieties of fruit, and stuck to them loyally. In Cottenham, the apples Jolly Miller and Murfitts Seedling were grown and were seldom seen in 'foreign' orchards, although Radford Beauty, a Cottenham variety, was also grown at Impington and Histon. The favourites in Histon were Barton and Colwell, while John Norman was another exclusive Cottenham variety.

Plums seemed to be less parochial and good old varieties such as Black Jack, Wheaten and Rye, were found all over the area.

Willingham strawberries were the first on the market in most seasons; they grew Joseph Paxton and, later, the delicious and still popular Royal Sovereign. At Cottenham the still well-known families of Gautry and Thoday grew soft fruit; by 1894, Thoday had two acres of outdoor tomatoes, as well as some growing under glass.

At the turn of the century, flowers were in demand, as well as the more exotic vegetables; acres of land around Willingham, Rampton and Cottenham were put down to pyrethrums and chrysanthemums and quite thriving businesses were built around asparagus production. One curious crop, almost exclusively from Willingham, was early mint, grown from rhizomes under glass. These traditional crops are still grown today and many small plots of flowers can be seen on the outskirts of the now expanding villages.

The fruit-producing area around Wisbech grew up in just the same way as its southern counterpart. Kentish immigrants settled around the town at the end of the nineteenth century and vigorously expanded the small beginnings of the local growers. The first orchards were those of H H Bath and J Cockett. Cockett began in 1850; his apples were shaken off the trees and sent to the north of England by coaster. Bath was the largest grower in the area, having over 600 acres of vegetables, flowers and fruit by 1890. He employed over a thousand pickers during the strawberry season and grew pansy and violet plants for sale, over 100,000 of these being packed and sent away in a single day.

Jam factories were set up in the area, and besides apples and strawberries, gooseberries appeared to have been grown for their pectin which helped to set jam made from the other fruits. A famous local apple, Emneth Early, was introduced in 1899; Ayers and Newlings of Upwell and Outwell were the first to plant the still popular Bramley's Seedling, Newton Wonder, Lord Derby and Worcester Pearmain apples.

Perhaps the most spectacular and best known horticultural industry is Fenland bulb growing. In 1885, there was one bulb grower listed in a directory of Spalding— Mrs Quincey. By 1892 there were 75, over half of them being from Spalding itself. Mrs Quincey began by growing snowdrops and then narcissi. It was a time when the middle classes of Britain became interested in flower gardening and the bulb boom was on. J T White of Wisbech was one of the earliest growers; he collected bulbs as a hobby and sold them to retail outlets. Sensing the possibilities, he rented land at Spalding and set off on a new career. J and H Gostelow may have been the first to market bulb flowers, beginning by sending narcissi in an old hat box to Covent Garden. Richard Wellband was another pioneer, competing against the Dutch daffodil producers at Covent Garden in 1890. Within three years, he was forcing daffodils under glass. Fred Culpin was also among the first bulb producers, introducing Darwin tulips and Bath's Flame daffodils to the area.

Further north, at Frampton, Barker and Brown in 1882, were early fruit and flower growers and, at Swineshead, W W Johnson specialised in gooseberry production.

Actual acreages on which small fruit was grown can be gleaned from published agricultural statistics. From very small beginnings in the 1880s, fruit entered its boom years, by 1891 covering 2,000 acres in Cambridge-shire and the Isle of Ely (not all on the fens, of course) and 1,300 acres of Holland, Lincolnshire. In the next ten years, fruit reached a peak acreage of 3,500 and 1,700 in the two counties and then began to decline. Today the acreage is almost exactly that of 1891.

Bulbs really count as the Fenland success story. From the widespread but small acreages of the pre-war years, bulb crops increased to 3,000 acres in Holland by 1950 and in another 10 years had trebled that figure to become the biggest horticultural moneyspinner in the county, accounting for upwards of 30 per cent of farm output. The acreage and value of bulbs is now being steadily overtaken by cereals.

Vegetable crops are also increasing and now cover 50,000 acres in Holland and 25,000 in Cambridgeshire.

Fenland Agriculture Today

We have seen how the pattern of Fenland farming has changed from the mixed livestock and cropping regime of a century ago to almost total reliance on crop production today: current estimates are that only about 10 per cent of farm income in the Fens is derived from livestock or livestock products. What has not changed significantly is the size of the farm holdings. The slow change from small to large holdings that is taking place countrywide is reflected to some extent in the Fens, but there is still a very large number of farms of around 50 acres or less, each producing a high output of valuable horticultural crops and quite capable of supporting their occupiers. Even the few very large farm estates of over 1,000 acres almost invariably include a proportion of horticultural crops among their acreage.

Change and progress are the essence of farming the world over and Fenland farmers are among the most progressive, probably made so by the necessity to alter their methods of husbandry to accommodate the changes that are affecting their raw material, the soil. Before drainage, the peat fens were some six to twelve feet above the seaward siltlands, but they now lie below the silt level. Apart from the obvious drainage difficulties involved, this means that the Fenland consists of three soil types rather than the simple peat and silt duo; for the shrinkage of the peat has exposed the underlying subsoil to form a third typical fen soil type: the skirtlands. Already some 100,000 acres of fen have lost their peat cover and now consist of admixtures of sand or clay and silt—mixtures that can be of low fertility or extremely difficult to work.

Thus areas that were for many years highly suited to production of clean, well-shaped root vegetables, such as carrots, have been lost and the Fenland farmer has had to adapt his methods, or his cropping, to manage an entirely new soil type.

191

It is necessary here to correct one fairly widespread misconception: the peat has not disappeared by being blown away in dust storms. This does occur, but the actual loss of soil in this manner is minute, most of it being deposited in the next field or dyke. The danger of a fen blow is in the loss of seed and fertiliser and most of all in the damage that the sharp particles of peat and sand do to tender young seedlings. If the sugar beet seed is blown away, it is easy enough, apart from the extra expense, to drill some more. But if the seed has had time to germinate and produce a plant, it is likely that the new drilling will be at least a month behindhand: in farming time is money and at harvest the late-drilled crop will yield only half its potential.

The most important effect of all is the physical loss of bulk during hydro-contraction following drainage; much of this occurred relatively quickly after the first drainage of the fens. Nowadays the action of bacteria on the organic material within the soil, and oxidation caused by the activating effect of constant tillage inherent in continuous arable cropping, is probably the cause of the regular 1in a year drop in peat levels.

Those farmers already on skirtland have adapted their methods accordingly; where peat still exists, a new technique of soil mixing is being considered, whereby the remnants of the peat topsoil are diluted with the subsoil, producing a uniform rooting medium and hopefully arresting the final decay of the surface peat, while at the same time retaining benefits in terms of yield and in preserving an easily workable soil.

Other problems are posed by bog oaks and by roddons. The heavy trunks, not only of oaks, but firs, birches and alders, have been preserved in the peat and are gradually uncovered as the land surface shrinks downwards, making them liable to be hit by ploughs and cultivators. They then have to be dug out and dragged to the field edge, many being so large that they have to be cut up before they can be removed. As they have the consistency of wet tangled wire, this can be quite an exasperating and time-consuming job.

Roddons, being of silt and clay, cause problems in fen fields on account of their differing soil characteristics. When the rest of the field is just dry enough to work, the roddon will still be wet and sticky; conversely, where irrigation is applied to a growing crop, the peat soil will need a lot more water than that of the roddon. The impeded drainage of the roddon can also lead to problems within the crop; the course of the silt bank can often be followed in a standing crop of wheat by noting the incidence of take-all, a root disease of cereals which is encouraged by sticky soil conditions and which can lead to almost complete loss of yield in affected plants. As a purely physical problem, the clay of a roddon might stick to celery or carrots and render them almost impossible to clean for sale.

Along the Breckland edge, the fen soil is often mixed with underlying or blown sand, forming a typical hummock and hollow scenery. This type of land is extremely difficult to farm successfully, suffering as it does from successive waterlogging ar ' drought, constantly in danger of blowing during any dry spell. Much of the land is down to grass, which provides rough grazing, or is covered by plantations of poplar trees, grown for matchwood.

One other problem is particularly important on the highly fertile peat. Because of its very fertility, it is not only crops that grow strongly and yield well; any land left untended, even for a few days in spring and summer, will very quickly be covered by a lush mat of weed growth, with nettles, redshank, even sedge and reed, springing up almost overnight it seems. The high organic content of the soil has led to many problems in the development of successful herbicides and special chemicals are needed on the peat. Without these aids, modern intensive farming, relying on low numbers of workers, would be impossible.

FENLAND AGRICULTURE

The alluvial silts in the northern Fens are as highly fertile as the peatlands in their own way and pose their own particular problems, not of contraction of blowing, but of structure loss and compaction. Almost all the silt soils in the region are seriously lacking in organic matter. They have not always been so, for less than 100 years ago, when much of the area was grass-covered grazing land, the organic content was sufficient to promote an excellent structure within the soil. The early arable farmers took advantage of this very stable soil and ploughed out almost the whole of the grassland; since then continuous arable cropping, without replacing the organic matter in the soil, has led to the present situation of a potentially very fertile soil giving below maximum yields. This results from loss of structure within the soil, which is unable to form a stable crumb, and leads to a number of conditions all contributing to yield loss. On such a soil, surface capping occurs regularly, preventing the emergence of small seedlings such as sugar-beet; the passing of heavy implements, or maybe just ploughing under slightly too wet conditions, leads to the formation of a concrete-like pan several inches below the surface, which restricts root development and water movement in dry spells and waterlogs the surface layer during rain.

There are methods of dealing with these problems: more and more farmers are putting down short-term grassland leys of three to four years to build up organic matter in their silt, and many fields are deep-busted after harvest using a very deep wedge or mole plough to break up the hard sub-surface pan.

From this it can be seen that merely to manage Fenland soils correctly is a very skilful job; to harvest continual high yields from the crops calls for husbandry of the highest order.

Fenland Crops

Despite the fact that very high value cash crops can be

194

seen all over the Fens, cereals—in particular autumn-sown wheats—now cover the largest acreage. Wheat fits in well with the rotations currently practised, acting almost as a break or land-resting crop between years of potato, sugar-beet and vegetables. Very heavy yields of grain can be obtained from well-managed silts; for a variety of reasons, some poorly understood, the yield and quality of autumn-sown wheat from the peats are often rather disappointing. It may be that the crop suffers from a deficiency of those trace elements such as copper and manganese that are lacking in the peat soils, although spray applications of these minerals are often given to many crops.

Where the ground is occupied by late maturing crops, such as carrots and maincrop potatoes, fields may not be ready in time for autumn sowing; therefore, spring wheat is grown, usually very successfully, on the peat, where its yield often surpasses that of autumn-sown crops. Again, this anomaly is not fully understood, although it is possibly because the soft black earth heaves during a hard frost, which exposes and breaks the stem bases and roots of autumn-sown wheats. The spring-sown wheat would, of course, usually escape this setback.

Barley is grown on the silt and skirt soils, but is not so popular on the deepest peats, where the highly nitrogenous organic content produces a tall and lank-growing plant which lodges or topples over before harvest, leading to uneven ripening, sprouting of wet grain and a difficult pick-up for the combine harvester. Smallholders who also run a small pig enterprise often sow an acre or two for home milling their own feed-meal.

Cereal growing is completely mechanised, from the first seed bed preparation to final combine harvesting. Perhaps the only hand work required is in a field of corn grown for seed production, where a thoroughly clean sample is required. In this case a team of roguers will comb the field pulling out weeds, especially wild oats, before harvest. It is a tiring job, now being made slightly easier by the introduction of a killer glove which injects a small quantity of herbicide as each wild oat is gripped by the glove.

Potatoes

Potatoes are still the basis of Fenland farming, with around 36 per cent of the country's main crop coming from the area. Some earlies are grown on the silts, but the Fens cannot compete for climate with Cornwall and Dyfed; the main crop varieties of King Edward, Majestic, Pentland Crown, etc can all be lifted as soon as the cereal harvest permits. Potatoes require great expertise in husbandry, such simple requirements as the spacing of seed tubers along the row and the width of each row needing to be worked out exactly. The crop requires so much in the way of subsequent cultivation and spraying that row widths must correspond to the width of tractor wheels and implements.

Once the potatoes have grown too large to be tractor-hoed without damage, some crops may be hand-hoed once or twice, though residual herbicides do keep this work down to a minimum. In July regular spraying to prevent the epidemic spread of the fungus disease, potato blight, begins. The fungus requires warm humid weather to multiply and, throughout the Fens, weather conditions are monitored to provide a warning system for the onset of blight attacks.

When the crop is close to harvest, the foliage is often burnt off using desiccating chemicals to prevent the tough haulm blocking the mechanical lifters and harvesters. All lifting is mechanised to some degree, though this varies from a simple plough share and elevator-cleaner which delivers the exposed tubers back onto the ground for subsequent collection, to sophisticated machines which deliver a clean sample of potatoes into a trailer ready for carting off. Much of the picking up of potatoes from the broken open ridges is done by gangs, either of local women and casual labourers or of itinerant families who migrate into the Fens in trailers and caravans at that time of year.

Some of the produce is bagged and sold straight away, but thousands of tons are stored in earth and straw clamps by the roadside, in straw bale pies or, increasingly, in controlled environment stores, where conditions can be regulated to keep the crop in good condition for sale into the spring of the next year. Even in non-controlled storage, sprout suppressants can be applied to the tubers to stop vegetative growth when the atmosphere warms up.

Before sale, potatoes are usually riddled out of clamp or store, going over a grader, where all damaged or diseased tubers can be removed before bagging up. It is a feature of the winter landscape to see gangs of riddlers at work, sheltered in part by polythene covered shelters, or to find oneself stuck along miles of narrow road behind the huge lorries that carry the produce to market.

On potato growing farms, there is often a large glass-house used to raise a few tomatoes in the summer but really a chitting house, where seed potatoes bought in from Scotland or Ireland can be boxed up in late winter, given artificial light and some heat to keep them frost-free and their eyes opened to produce small chits or sprouts before planting begins. This enables the potatoes to grow away quickly in the soil and heavier yields result.

Very few home-grown potatoes are saved for seed because the relatively warm conditions in the Fens encourage the spread of aphids in the growing crop. The aphids carry and spread several quite severe viruses which can affect the potato and lower its yield, so most seed is obtained from colder areas, where spread of the virus diseases is less likely to occur.

Potato growing has been restricted in recent years by a very damaging and prevalent pest—the potato cyst eelworm—which appears wherever too many potatoes are grown with insufficient break. There are now ways of combating this pest, either by the use of very efficient but expensive nematicides, or by growing one of the varieties, such as Maris Piper, which are resistant to some strains of the eelworm.

Potatoes produce a lot of colour in the green mid-summer fens; Maris Piper throws up a haze of purple flowers, while the Pentland varieties and Majestics give white flowers. The bulb fields do not have it all their own way!

Yields are usually high, and well up to the average for the country of 12 tons per acre.

Sugar-beet

Sugar-beet is grown under contract from the British Sugar Corporation who own the region's beet sugar factories at Ely, Peterborough, Spalding, Wissington and King's Lynn. The acreage covered on the peat is similar to that of potatoes, but is slightly lower in the traditional potato lands of Lincolnshire. Again, it is a crop eminently suited to the rotation, soils and available expertise of the Fens. Once requiring an enormous labour force, its production is now highly mechanised, from precision-spaced drilling of single seed pellets to machine lifting.

The seed of sugar-beet is compound, that is several seeds occur together in a clump, and it was not until the advent of rubbed seed giving a single seed unit, and the encasing of this monogerm within a round seed pellet of absorbent material, that the onerous task of hand singling the seedling crop could be minimised. For sugar-beet need space in which to grow, and if there are too many plants, too close together, then small roots and a low yield result.

Despite modern precision drills and the use of herbicides, hand-hoeing is still usually required at least once to remove close spaced seedlings and the tougher weeds. This back-breaking task again provides work for the itinerant gangs during the early summer and also some hard-earned evening perks for the locals.

Rotation of the crop is rigorously controlled by the British Sugar Corporation to prevent the spread of eelworm pests. The other main enemies of sugar-beet are aphids which migrate on to the crop in early summer, carrying the virus disease yellows which, as its name implies, reduces the available green area of leaf, thus cutting down the weight and sugar yields from the crop. An early warning system is operated by fieldsmen and research workers to enable growers to forestall the aphids by an application of insecticide.

Harvest is still known as the campaign and begins in October, when the factories open for delivery of beet. Years ago much of the beet was delivered from the farm by barge or railway truck, the larger farms often being served by a little single track railway merely to take the beet harvest. Nowadays the harvest travels by lorry, and each grower is issued with a code which tells him on which days he may deliver his beet to the factory and on which days there is free-loading when anyone can deliver. Samples of beet are taken from each lorry and the grower is paid according to the sugar content of his beet and the dirt tare of each load. The sugar content varies according to sunshine, rainfall, soil and other factors; it often happens that a hot, dry season will produce small roots with a high proportion of sugar and, a cool wet year, large roots with a lower proportion. Actual figures for sugar content vary between 11–12 per cent early in the season to 15–16 per cent later on.

The campaign goes on until all, or nearly all, the beet is harvested. In exceptional years, such as 1974, really wet conditions can bog down the heavy harvesting machinery and stop the campaign altogether in mid-season, but this is a very rare occurrence. During the season, huge piles of beet are accumulated, often sited by the roadside on hard stands, waiting to be carted into the factories. The crop is usually all taken in by February.

Large-scale Horticulture

We come now to what may be termed the growing of horticultural crops on an agricultural scale. In most parts of Britain, the growing of onions, carrots, lettuce, cauliflowers and soft fruit is more-or-less the occupation of gardeners and smallholders; in the Fens it is big business, with each crop in its traditional area, although the areas are becoming less well defined.

The silts are predominantly fruit and brassicae areas, Wisbech being the centre of a large fruit growing area which extends well into Norfolk and northwards into Lincolnshire. The deep silts are ideal for strawberries, the principal soft fruit crop, as even a small acreage of the crop can create a viable unit; thus we find an exceptionally large proportion of very small holdings in this region. The plants are grown in matted rows, that is they are allowed to grow together along each row, but with a clear space between rows; they are cropped usually for three seasons, about one-third of the acreage of each holding being grubbed up each year and replaced elsewhere. Rotation must be practised to avoid the risk of soil-borne disease.

Although the use of residual herbicides has simplified the spring work load on a strawberry holding, enormous numbers of pickers are required during the three weeks or so of harvest; huge international camps of pickers, mainly students, have been formed, like the one at Friday Bridge and the fens are crowded with the caravans of travelling gangs.

The first pickings are carefully boxed for the fresh fruit market, but later the fruit is picked plugged, with no calyx, boxed and sent by the lorry load to processing factories for canning and jam-making. It is a short, sharp, colourful season, with hard money being earned and few fortunes made. Some strawberries, and also gooseberries, are still grown in the southern Fens in the traditional fruit area of Cottenham, which is otherwise more of a top fruit area.

Gooseberries are also important around Wisbech, often being grown between rows of Bramley apples; the huge old Bramleys are pruned to a low, spreading shape, originally designed to match the capacity of the low-power spraying machines available at the time when the orchards were first begun.

Cauliflowers, with some brussels sprouts, are grown in large quantities on the silts bordering the Wash. Successive crops are raised under glass and planted out on a field scale to mature; pest control is very important, especially in the summer cauliflowers where one caterpillar can make for a lot of consumer resistance. Spacing of plants and fertiliser application are absolutely critical for the production of a first-class crop, as often only the top-quality produce gains a profitable market. Harvesting is still largely by hand: cutting cauliflowers in June can be quite a pleasant job, picking sprouts in December is best left to the imagination.

The sticky silt soils are difficult to remove from root vegetables and, although the acreage of onions on the silts is increasing, it is on the lighter soils in the south that we find root vegetables growing at their best. These high-value crops can again provide a viable holding on a small acreage, and a large proportion are under 50 acres.

Chatteris is the carrot centre of Britain. Originally the hub of an actual growing area, it is still the headquarters of the carrot trade with a number of growers and merchants operating from the town and growing the crop on contract as far away as the light sand-lands of Norfolk, around Swaffham. Some early carrots are grown, perhaps with irrigation, for the summer market, but the main trade is for mature carrots, harvested from September to the following April, for winter sale. Many are left in the ground, sometimes protected by straw, throughout the winter, to be harvested when weather and markets dictate. A constant supply is required by the canners, pre-packers and soup makers, and all produce needs to be uniform in size and of excellent quality. Size of root is governed initially by seed rate, and a grower needs to be sure what market he is aiming for even before the crop is sown. Insecticide application to prevent the ravages of carrot root fly, and attention to rotation, are very important if high quality is to be achieved. Carrots are steam-peeled in processing and any blemishes remaining are liable to lead to rejection of that grower's next load.

Celery is a whole Fenland industry in itself; over 100 million seedlings are raised under glass around Whittlesey and pricked out in nursery beds during early spring (Pl 22, p 174). They are then planted out on the peat fields around Ely, Littleport and Southery to be harvested during autumn and winter. Over three quarters of all Britain's celery is grown there, the soil being absolutely perfect for the crop and the skilled labour still readily available.

The crop is planted out in wide rows partly by machine, partly by hand, and ridged up later to blanch the stems. Harvesting is a slow process, with some machinery being used. Most of the crop is cleared by December, but some deeply-ridged crops are not lifted until early in the new year. Celery lifted in prime condition is now being kept in cool store for up to two months before being put on the market, enabling the grower to take advantage of good harvesting weather and to catch a better market later in the season.

An enormous tonnage of onions is imported into Britain each year and it is the aim of Fen growers to see this reduced. Onions, grown and prepared properly, can be a very lucrative crop, the emphasis being on quality, to enable our home produce to compete with the Spanish imports. Once again precision drilling, residual herbicides and better harvesting machinery are gradually reducing the need for a lot of hand labour in growing this crop. Hand-hoeing must still be done on many fields and harvesting and riddling do take quite a labour force still.

Some onions are now being sown in August to stand the winter and be ready for harvest in late June, thus catching a market previously available only to imported produce. The newer Japanese varieties are particularly suitable for this treatment. But the vast majority of onions are drilled as early in the spring as possible and harvested from late August onwards. New techniques of dry, warm storage, giving the crop a curing period of heat treatment, are producing a well matured onion, with a golden, attractive skin. The old method was to leave the crop on the field to dry amid the vagaries of an English autumn and to store it in a vast damp heap, a process guaranteed to produce split, spoiled and diseased onions. A new method of treating the seed chemically is also lessening the incidence of one of the fungus diseases which cause rotting of the onions in store.

The rather specialised technique of growing small onions for the pickling trade has been taken up by farmers around Southery, where a processing plant has been installed as a co-operative venture.

Many other vegetable crops are grown: lettuces, leeks, beetroot and parsnips are all grown on a field scale and Dutch White cabbage, dwarf beans and turnips also find a place in the varied enterprises of the Fens. There is a considerable acreage of chicory, a crop which resembles sugar-beet and is taken to similar factories, at St Ives and Lakenheath, for drying to be used as a coffee additive.

Bulbs and Flowers

We have dealt first, quite rightly, with edible crops but the Fens are just as famous, if not more so, for the quality and quantity of the ornamental stock produced, particularly bulbs. The annual Spalding Bulb Festival, when millions of tulips are in bloom around the town, is now an international event. The exhibition at Spring-fields, the Spalding show nursery belonging to the bulb growing trade, provides a wonderful shop window for the industry.

The flowering year begins with the production of daffodil and tulip blooms before Christmas, under heated glass. The bulbs that are to be forced are grown in the previous season on the usual field scale, out of doors; tulips are lifted out of the ground at the end of June and daffodils during July. The grower then needs to know exactly how many flowers he is going to produce for each date, because the treatment to which the bulb is subjected after lifting will govern its behaviour under forcing conditions. For instance, tulip bulbs that are required to bloom before Christmas must be kept at a temperature of 20°C (68°F) after lifting. During this time a few bulbs must be cut to examine the development of the flower shoot inside the bulb. When a certain stage is reached the temperature is lowered to 17°C (63°F) for a further week or two to complete the flower develop-ment, after which the bulbs are cool stored at 9°C (48°F) until planting commences at the end of September. Sometimes the bulbs are kept at temperatures as high as 25°C (78°F) for a week after lifting, to hasten the initiation of the flower inside the bulbs.

Bulbs that are required to flower at later dates receive slightly different treatment in the way of storage temperature and length of time held at each heat. Growing to such blueprint methods has been perfected in the Netherlands and Fenland growers have taken the techniques, modified them for their own requirements, and are now producing very high quality forced blooms during late December to March, when there are few other flowers in the shops.

In spring some outdoor daffodils are harvested for

sale as cut blooms, followed a week or two later by the tulips. But flowers are not the main crop from field grown bulbs; it is the bulb itself which is lifted when mature and sold. Small daffodil bulbs are planted during September and October and left to grow for two seasons. During that time the flowers are removed before running to seed, to improve the size of the bulb. In the second summer after planting, the bulbs are lifted, dried and graded out for sale into mother bulbs, or broodies, which have several growing points or noses, each capable of producing flower stems, double-nosed, or rounds which have only one growing point. The smaller offsets, or chips, are retained for growing on as planting stocks. In 1974, the yield of daffodil bulbs from the Lincolnshire silts was around 27,000 tonnes.

In spite of the large daffodil production it is the tulip which has become the emblem of Fenland bulb fields. Young tulip bulbs are planted out in early autumn and are grown on for only one year, being lifted for sale in the following June or July. The glorious sight of tulip fields in spring draws crowds into the Spalding area from many parts of Britain and abroad: special routes are marked out through the lanes and villages to show off all the best of the dusty pink, red and yellow acres. However, the spectacle is short-lived, for, like the daffodils, the tulip must be beheaded if a good yield of bulbs is to be obtained. Nor must the flower stalk be cut off, since its photosynthetic material helps to feed the bulb during its growing period.

Millions of the tulip flowers are used to decorate the intricate and marvellous floats that parade through the town during the Spalding Bulb Festival, but many millions more end up in dumps and dyke sides. Again, in 1974, 650 million tulip bulbs were produced in the Holland part of Lincolnshire. In all, something over 10,000 acres of bulbs are grown in the Fens, and this includes gladioli and iris, which are grown for sale as cut flowers, both under glass and in the field.

Other flower crops include peonies, freesia and pyrethrums. Quite large wholesale businesses, with nursery trade outlets, are found in the Wisbech area and also on the eastern side of the peat Fens, where trees, shrubs and fruit stocks are grown.

Of other ornamental stock enterprises, there is the expanding business of rose growing around Wisbech, which is fast building itself a national reputation, and the glasshouse industry of the Spalding area which produces flowers and plants for the home, both catering for an expanding demand from leisure gardeners throughout Britain.

Visitors to Fenland often comment on the lack of livestock. There are some, but they are few and far between: in the peatlands, the fen islands and the washes are the only traditional grazing areas. Peat farmers reckon that the heavy land of the islands is only good for grass. There are still one or two dairy herds but most are single-suckling herds with indoor bullock yards for winter fattening. The washlands of the Ouse and Nene are used for summer grazing of cattle, with some sheep flocks, although these are not common. The Black Fens are best known for pigs, which being housed are not often seen. There are many excellent specialist breeding or fattening enterprises, which add considerably to the importance of the region agriculturally but take up little actual land.

Some farmers have shown interest in preserving the heavy horses once famous in the Fens. Farms at Willingham, Stuntney and Pymore, for instance, all keep championship studs of Percheron or Shire draught horses.

As more siltland is rested with a grass ley, so more and more sheep are to be found in that area; not enough to call it sheep country though it is no surprise to come across grazing flocks by the Welland, or across the Holbeach Marsh—they do make a welcome change from potatoes and wheat.

Plate 23 (above) The great brick keep of Tattershall Castle, seen from the west. In the background, across the moat and inner ward, is Lord Cromwell's collegiate church (*The National Trust*)

Plate 24 (below) Redbrick and stone trim at Frampton Hall. The main block was built in 1725 and is especially noted for the gorgeous rainwater heads on the north front (*D. Beard*)

Plate 25 Montagu's Harrier and young. The species once bred at Wicken but is now only a rare visitor there (*The National Trust*)

For the future of Fenland agriculture, it seems that the extra profit now available from cereal growing might attract more growers away from the unpredictable profitability of bulbs, potatoes, or even sugar-beet if the right contract cannot be found. Yet the need for more home-produced sugar is undeniable. Root crops on the diminishing peat are obviously becoming more difficult and may well be restricted to a few small areas within the next ten years. These crops again are likely to be replaced by cereals, as the risk of soil-borne diseases, which can be a limiting factor on organic soils, diminishes along with the peat.

Fenland agriculture has never stood still and no doubt will change to accommodate new problems, economic or practical. The region is well served by Ministry of Agriculture research farms at Mepal, on shallow peat, at Terrington St Clement, on the silts, and by the experimental horticultural station at Kirton. New ideas and new techniques are constantly appearing; Fenland agriculture will surely be in a healthy state for many years to come.

11 The Natural History
of the Fens

Introduction

WE have seen how the Fenland is one of the most intensively cultivated areas in Britain and popular opinion might well equate this with sprays, pesticides and a barren environment; it might be thought that the strict husbandry of the fens would lead to their being one huge open-air factory for corn, potatoes and clinically clean orchards. In fact, the fens are, in human terms, relatively empty and free from the disturbing influences of industry and towns. The result is that the area supports wild life in as many rich and varied forms as any other 'tamed' landscape in the country.

The isolation of the fens is easy to experience, even at the height of summer when the clatter of combine harvesters and constant traffic of tractors seem to fit in with the wide landscape and fade into insignificance. The actual disturbance caused by most agricultural processes on the fens is minimal, so easily do the tractor and cultivator fit into the natural order.

It need not be imagined that every acre of available land is cultivated; although trees and hedges are perhaps rather thinly scattered they do exist and are densely colonised by birds, animals and plants that prefer such an environment. Water is to be found everywhere, and the smallest farm dyke provides a bank habitat of grasses and scrub, while the wider drains and rivers, some of them tidal, often include mud and marsh habitats. Many fields far from the isolated farmhouses are connected by wide green lanes, the fen droves, which hold a rich, often largely undisturbed, flora and fauna. Farmyards and buildings themselves offer nesting places for birds, more often than not including a patch or two of nettles and scrub around the back of the barn where insects can breed.

All this constitutes the 'tamed' landscape of Fenland, a landscape which, although not yet desperately threatened by the urbanisation and development which is smothering much of southern Britain, has nevertheless had to adapt to the needs and practices of a successful modern business. In contrast to this vast cultivated tract, the Fenland also contains some of the most wild and attractive areas that can be found in lowland Britain.

The Ouse Washes, between the two Bedford rivers, have become one of the most interesting, and certainly one of the most important, wetland nature reserves in Europe. At Wicken Fen, only a few miles from Cambridge, is a remnant of old fen vegetation; a nature reserve which shows us what botanical succession is all about and gives a glimpse of the old fen conditions. Other fen reserves, at Wood Walton and Holme, have a different story to tell, having developed from an acid bog community into a complex pattern of acid and alkali vegetation, culminating in fen and carr, such as is found at Wicken. At Chippenham Fen a wide variety of habitat again affords comparison with Wicken.

The silt marshes reach the sea around the Wash, where saltmarsh and sandbank provide a habitat for sea birds, seals and salt-loving plants.

Those who seek an annotated list of species to be found, or that have been discovered in the Fens, will find it easily available in the various Natural History reports that cover the area. Most people will want to know where they can go to begin finding out for themselves what there is to see. We shall therefore describe briefly what is happening to the various natural populations of the fens and what is being done to ensure that birds, animals and plants are looked after and encouraged. It would be pointless to try to explain in detail what the visitor might see; anything can happen on the fens, and sometimes does! Jeremy Sorenson, formerly Royal Society for the Protection of Birds warden on the Ouse Washes, tells of a Red Kite being mobbed by a breeding pair of Black Tailed Godwits, and of a Bittern walking up his drive. At Wicken, probably the most intensively research-ed and documented reserve in the country (with the exception of Monks Wood, near Huntingdon), previously unrecorded insect species are still turning up regularly.

Fenland Nature Reserves

Nature conservation in the Fens is undertaken jointly by the state and by national and local voluntary organisa-tions. The oldest conservation society, the Royal Society for the Protection of Birds, was the first to recognise the tremendous importance of the Ouse Washes as a wetland breeding and overwintering site; it now owns and administers a large proportion of the washes. The National Trust owns Wicken Fen for the nation. The Wildfowl Trust, the research and conservation body set up by Sir Peter Scott, also owns part of the Ouse Washes and has built a most impressive series of lagoons, with hidden access to an observatory where members of the public can watch wildfowl and waders in comfort. The Nature Conservancy Council maintains, as National Nature Reserves, Wood Walton and Holme Fens and Chippenham Fen. Of the local voluntary organisations, the Cambridgeshire and Isle of Ely Naturalists' Trust (known, for understandable reasons of brevity, as Cambient) owns a further share of the Ouse Washes, as does the Bedfordshire and Huntingdon-shire Naturalists' Trust. In the north, the observatory at

Gibraltar Point is administered by the Lincolnshire Naturalists' Trust.

Wicken Fen

The nature reserve of Wicken Fen lies at the head of Wicken Lode, just to the south of the village of that name, about 10 miles north of Cambridge. The fen was long thought to be a last example of natural fen vegetation, but in the 1920s the work of Sir Harry Godwin, who demonstrated the fen succession from open water to native woodland carr, showed the fallacy of this belief. Within such a hydrosere succession, there could be no niche for many of the plant species found at Wicken, and only when some disturbance interrupted the succession could colonisation by such species take place. In fact, it was the cessation of practices like peat digging and sedge cutting, rather than the actual carrying on of such work, that caused the rare local plant life to decline during this century.

For perhaps hundreds of years, the villagers of Wicken had owned strips of Wicken Sedge Fen, still marked today by metal posts. From their strips they had mown sedge (*Cladium moriscum*) to be used as cattle litter or thatch. The frequency of the mowing would vary with need and thus has produced a pattern of vegetation showing differing proportions of reeds, sedge and grasses. On other strips, peat would be dug for fuel, leaving a bare peat surface subject to seasonal flooding—an ideal habitat for such plants as the fen violet (*Viola stagnina*).

This is one of the most famous of the fenland species and is still to be found at Wood Walton Fen. Once common at Wicken, by the early part of this century the fen violet had become extinct there. Studies of the plant at Wood Walton have shown that it is a species that survives best on open peat subject to seasonal winter flooding and dry summer conditions. Its seeds will lie dormant in the peat until suitable conditions appear. The fen violet obviously thrived at Wicken during the period when peat digging was taking place; when this ceased, its open habitat was gradually lost and the species declined and was finally lost to the site.

Similarly, the insect life of the reserve must at one time have been even richer than it is today, since, under the conditions of differing human interference, a great range of peatland habitats could be found which supported a correspondingly large variety of organisms. When such disturbance ceased the fen gradually reverted to a more uniform habitat, with a consequent reduction in the variety of plant and animal life.

The fen today consists of three areas: Sedge Fen, Adventurer's Fen and St Edmund's Fen, about 700 acres in all. The peat in the surrounding arable fenland has shrunk and been lost following drainage and cultivation and is now up to 8ft below the level of Wicken Sedge Fen. This lowering of the water level around the reserve has obviously affected the habitats within it almost as much as the changes in human disturbance which have occurred during the same period. The drier conditions were much more suited to the spread of Alder Buckthorn (*Frangula alnus*) from the margin of the fen into the reserve itself. Today the water level is kept artificially high by the operation of sluice gates; management is being directed towards removing some of the dense carr of Alder Buckthorn, Buckthorn (*Rhamnus catharticus*) and Guelder Rose (*Viburnum opulus*) which covers much of the fen. If left untouched, the carr areas would be succeeded eventually by either Oak–Ash, or Birch woodlands and already, in some of the older carrs, a mature woodland, with a field-layer of Marsh Fern (*Thelypteris palustris*) and other shade tolerant plants such as Dewberry (*Rubus caesius*), is developing. It is planned to re-establish productive sedge fields in order, once again, to provide a variety of habitats within the reserve and already the sedge is cropped regularly every three to four years and the bundles shipped out along Wicken Lode to be used for thatching.

One of the most exciting developments in recent years has been the digging of a 10-acre mere on Adventurer's Fen in 1954–55. This secluded site has been a great success; open water species are now attracted into the reserve, and fourteen species of duck have been recorded there. Great Crested Grebe, Bearded Tit and Bittern are all seen regularly and in winter up to 1,000 Mallard, 70 Pochard, 500 Teal, 400 Wigeon and 80 Pintail visit the mere and can be watched without disturbance from the stilt hide built on the Sedge Fen bank.

The Wicken Fen Group has been trapping and ringing birds of the sedge fields and carr for several years: between 1968 and 1973 they captured and ringed 18,500 birds of over 70 species ranging from the Long-eared Owl to the Goldcrest. Their work is not solely concerned with ringing for migration and age studies, although these are obviously of great interest, as valuable data on body-weight, wing length, state of moulting and presence or absence of brood patch have been recorded. Even the time of day of each capture is noted to provide information on the differing activity periods in, for example, the male and female Blackcap which share incubation of the eggs.

Saturation trapping of given sites on the reserve at certain set dates for several consecutive years has provided data on population changes: from 1970 to 1973 the Bullfinch population more than doubled, while over the same period the number of Sedge Warblers has more than halved. The most common species trapped is the Reed Warbler.

Probably the best-known inhabitant of Wicken Fen is the Swallowtail butterfly, which at one time bred on the reserve. Around 1950 the resident population died out and any specimen now seen flying during June over the sedge fields and droves will have been imported from

Norfolk-derived laboratory stock. The demise of this typical fen insect is probably related to the reduction in the area of sedge field on the reserve, coupled with the associated increase in carr. Food plants for the caterpillars have decreased and the lack of nectar flowers for the adults has adversely affected their environment. Nor must we forget that over-collecting of all stages of the insect probably contributed to its extinction on this site. It remains to be seen whether the attempt to re-introduce the species will succeed; a previous experiment during the 1930s to bring in a 'foreign' race of the Large Copper butterfly, then extinct in the Fens, was a dismal failure.

Other species once recorded at Wicken and no longer to be seen are the Large Tortoiseshell and the Dark Green Fritillary. On the other hand, species such as the Holly Blue, Comma and one or two of the Skippers seem to have colonised the fen during this century. One other typical fen species, the Brimstone, is quite common at Wicken.

We have seen that the Wicken Fen reserve is a place of continuous change, not static in any sense of the word. Management directed towards holding, and if possible increasing, the variety of habitat on the fen can only heighten its importance to naturalists and researchers. A well-informed public now presents its own management problems: literally thousands of visitors are coming to Wicken Fen every year to satisfy interests roused by school and adult educational courses and by televised natural history programmes. A modern unit, containing laboratory, teaching and display facilities, adds considerably to the educational possibilities of the area. Luckily the reserve is big enough to accommodate this influx without too much damage being done; in any case, many parts of the fen have had a long tradition of completely open access and it would be pointless to attempt to stop it now. Other areas, such as the mere, have been restricted in access right from the start, a policy that should prove beneficial as disturbance increases elsewhere and more and more people come to enjoy the fen.

The Ouse Washes

In 1965 the washlands between the Bedford rivers, then designated a Site of Special Scientific Importance, were described in a single paragraph in the British Association's book *The Cambridge Region* and concern was expressed about the ultimate fate of this most important marshland habitat. In the ten years since then, the accumulation of parcels of land within the Washes by conservation interests, the provision of full-time wardens, and specialised management of the reserves has provided the Fens with one of the most important wetland habitats in Europe, as well as a breeding area for several very rare and local bird species.

Long before conservation had ever been heard of, the Ouse Washes were a famous wildfowl haunt; generations of fen punt-gunners had eked out a living on the winter flood waters by shooting large numbers of the ducks, geese and swans that lived there. Old prints exist showing wildfowlers bringing home their catch, and it is certain that the winter economy of the fens was greatly dependent on the presence of so large a population of waterfowl more or less on the doorstep. But it was not really until the opening up of the fens during and after World War II that reliable statistics concerning wildfowl populations could be gleaned from the Washes. Until that time, many parts of the fens were still as remote as anywhere in the country; access was by boat or by way of almost impossibly muddy droveways. Sir Peter Scott, studying at Cambridge between the wars, was one of the few amateur sportsmen to shoot the Washes, covering the waters between Earith and Oxlode in a specially built punt.

The demands of wartime agriculture led to the construction of hard roads on both sides of the Bedford rivers during, or just after, the 1939–45 conflict, and an increasing interest in wildlife, coupled with the arrival of motor transport for all, meant that more and more attention was paid to the wild, remote vastness of the Washes. It was in the early 1950s that a local ornithologist first suspected the presence of breeding pairs of Black-tailed Godwits on the rough grazing land of the Welney Washes. This is a species that had not bred regularly in Britain for over a century but which had been increasing in numbers during the last twenty years. Young were first reared in 1952 and by 1958 a colony of nine pairs had been established. It was the beginning of one of the most exciting developments in the field of nature conservation seen in Britain.

The breeding of the Godwits was a jealously kept secret for several years. Under the protection of the Royal Society for the Protection of Birds, young were reared every year until in 1958 the time came to tell the world of this breeding success; even then the exact locality of the nesting was safeguarded and this did not, in fact, become general knowledge until early in the 1960s, after conservation interests had been able to assess the situation and to buy up or lease a considerable area of the Washland. It was the presence of the Godwits that focussed attention on the fact that here, in the heart of the Fens, was a large area of natural wilderness, having almost unlimited potential.

We have seen in Chapter 3 that the Ouse Washes are a man-made habitat, created out of the need for a large safety-valve reservoir that could hold flood water without fear of damage or loss to the surrounding countryside. The whole area is criss-crossed by a series of drainage dykes, breaking up the land into washes or rough water meadows of anything between 10 and 30 acres each. It is the traditional practice to use the meadows for summer grazing of cattle and sheep or to cut hay from the finer grasslands. In the autumn the stock is removed, leaving the washes to the vagaries of wind and water.

It is the maintenance of this traditional pattern of husbandry that is now so important to the preservation of the various habitats which make the washes attractive to breeding and over-wintering birds. As at Wicken Fen, it is human interference that has created the variety of habitat which in turn leads to the variety of flora and fauna. Heavy grazing of a wash followed by shallow winter flooding will create an ideal environment for wading birds, but will not provide enough food material to attract wildfowl. Rough washland, containing a number of semi-aquatic and grassland weed plants and left ungrazed so that seeding can take place, will provide food for the dabbling ducks and swans. Part-grazed wash consisting of tussocky grassland with perhaps some reed, is ideal breeding ground for certain species of wildfowl and waders, others preferring the privacy of long grass left for hay, or the open ground of well grazed marsh. Another small but nevertheless very important habitat produced by the normal agricultural activities on the washes, is that of the spoil-heaps left by drainage machines clearing out the dykes; in times of flood these heaps form long islands above the water and are very much used by waders and wildfowl as roosting places.

Added to these more or less natural habitats are the new, relatively deep-water lagoons that have been built by the Wildfowl Trust and the Royal Society for the Protection of Birds on their reserves; these lagoons have added tremendously to the attractions of the area for wildfowl.

The cessation of shooting over large areas of the washes following the formation of the wildfowl refuges has led to an increase in bird population. It is not so much the actual killing of wildfowl that reduces the population as the disturbance caused by the sportsmen themselves. Without roosting and feeding grounds that are relatively free from intrusion, there will never be large numbers of ducks and waders, which are among the shyest of birds.

The Black-tailed Godwits have certainly repaid the interest shown in them; from the small beginnings in the early 1960s, there are now up to 60 breeding pairs spread over several localities along the washes during most summers. From about the end of January onwards, the birds can be seen around the lagoons and shallow pools; in the breeding season proper, the washes are high with grasses and marsh plants so the birds are rather less conspicuous, until by the end of summer the family parties are once more forming into flocks.

Another famous breeding species that has been increasing recently is the Ruff. Early in the year their strange lekking display takes place, the males posturing to show off their often very individually coloured ruffs, like Elizabethan collars. Probably 30–40 pairs of these birds breed regularly on the reserves.

It is possible that another species will be added to the breeding list before very long: every year Black Terns are seen around the new lagoons and it is hoped that they will be persuaded to stay. Although there are few large reedbeds in the washes, the area seems more than suitable for the Bittern, which is seen in most winters and fairly regularly during summer; breeding could take place eventually.

These then are what we might call the regular rarities of summer on the washes; of course, the range of breeding species touches everything, from the small heronry to the relatively common Cuckoo and Turtle Dove. Reed Buntings and Yellow Hammers seem to be on the increase and are typical birds of the area; all the common finches, thrushes, and warblers abound, often finding suitable nesting sites in the isolated clumps and coppices of willow, alder and bramble. Many of the ducks and waders breed on the washes: among them quite large numbers of Mallard, Teal, Shoveler and

Tufted Duck, with smaller populations of Gadwall, Pochard and perhaps Wigeon. Snipe are probably the commonest breeding wader after the Lapwing, with upwards of 200 pairs; Redshank, Dunlin and Oyster-catchers can also be found.

Barn Owls are quite common all over Fenland and find the washes much to their liking, often nesting in old willow trunks; Tawny and Short-eared Owls are other regulars, while, on the sheltered summer waters of the Bedford rivers and the Delph river, Great-Crested and Little Grebes can be seen.

Many of the breeding birds, certainly the ducks and waders, have reared their young by high summer; July is the quietest month on the washes, with grasses and vegetation standing high across the dry meadows and the ducks quietly in eclipse. But by the end of the month, the wader passage has begun with migrating Green-shanks, Dunlin and Snipe arriving in ever increasing numbers. One of the features of this time of year is the concentration of Kestrels along the washes, the few breeding pairs being joined by up to 40 or more migrants, which it is believed come in from north-west England. On occasion, it is quite possible to see up to a dozen Kestrels all hovering within sight of one another. Really large numbers of hirundines pass through, up to 10,000 Sand Martins gathering in the osier beds before setting off south: Marsh Harriers are regular visitors and, by the end of September numbers of ducks, waders and Short-eared Owls are beginning to build up.

With the coming of winter, the washes really belong to the birds: in November the last of the cattle and sheep are removed and the only human activity is the digging out of drainage dykes. Nowadays this is done by one man and a machine, resulting in very little dis-turbance. In the old days, digging out by hand must have been a winter's work for quite large gangs of labourers.

Even if natural flooding does not occur, there are still

221

the lagoons providing much open water; they have been instrumental in attracting what is now the largest concentration of Bewick's Swans in Europe, a species which has become the symbol of the washes in winter. Up to 1,200 of these wonderful wild swans visit the reserves, many of them known individually to research workers at Welney, for their bill markings are infinitely variable. Whooper Swans can also be found, as well as the ubiquitous Mute.

Ducks, which have always been present in large numbers on the washes in winter, now reach truly amazing populations with the provision of the refuges. Well over 30,000 Wigeon is a regular estimate, with up to 7,000 Mallard, 1,000 Shoveler and large numbers of Tufted Duck, Pochard, Goldeneye and Gadwall. Many species are dependent upon weather conditions for their movements; Teal, for instance, a dabbling duck, dislike any period of high flood on the washes and flocks of well over 3,000 birds will disperse quickly under flood conditions. At certain times over a third of the total Pintail population of Great Britain can be found on the washes, with a flock of up to 2,000 visible from the public hides at Welches Dam. Numbers of this species in the locality have increased quite rapidly in the last twenty years.

Although the washes seem so suitable for geese very few are found there, only a few Greylag, Whitefront and Pink-footed Geese being seen in any year, with the very occasional Bean Goose. This is in strange contrast to the Nene Washes, only fifteen or so miles away as the goose flies, where quite large concentrations of roosting Pink-feet are found in times of flood.

Throughout the winter, the washes provide an important roost for the inland gull population of the fens. At its maximum, there are over 25,000 Black-headed Gulls, plus smaller numbers of Herring, Common and Great Black-backed Gulls roosting there, flighting in from agricultural land all around and from the sewage farms and rubbish tips of towns as far away as Newmarket and Cambridge. Other interesting regulars are flocks of Golden and Grey Plovers, Water Rails and up to twenty Short-eared Owls.

Wildfowling activities over the Washes have not stopped entirely, of course; by no means all the wash-land is in the hands of the conservation bodies, although agreement has been reached regarding shooting over quite a lot of the privately owned land. In some areas the traditionally independent mind of the Fenmen ensures that part of their way of life continues and it would surely be a pity if fen wildfowling did cease entirely in the area. In any case, very few of the winter duck population stays put on the refuges—large flocks of Mallard and Wigeon, for instance, flighting regularly out into the arable fields to feed. Some farmers have complained that damage is caused to winter crops by the duck; it is most unlikely that this is so as the birds feed mainly on small discarded potatoes from the crop preceding the wheat. Even where grazing of the young corn does take place, the final yield of the crop is likely to be as good as, or even better, than an untouched field. To many fen farmers the thought of fat ducks visiting their fields is enough to bring a gleam to the eye and set the trigger finger itching.

In the refuges research is continuing into the habits and preferences of wildfowl and waders, and already some of its results are being used in advising on the management of other wetland reserves, both in Britain and abroad. We have not mentioned the botany of the area, or the animal and insect life, all of which are worthy of consideration in their own right; but the washes are for the birds and disturbance is the one thing that they will not tolerate. Plant hunting or insect surveys are best left to the experts, for the washes are not the place for indiscriminate wanderers, however well-intentioned. To this end, specific bird-watching areas have been, and are being, set up. Public hides are available at Welches Dam and Purls Bridge on the western side of the washes on the Royal Society for the Protection of Birds reserve. The public is also admitted to the observatory of the Wildfowl Trust, north of Welney Suspension Bridge on the eastern side. The Cambridgeshire and Isle of Ely Naturalists' Trust also maintains hides overlooking its reserves, which are open to members only.

The wardens of the Royal Society for the Protection of Birds and the Wildfowl Trust conduct visits around their respective reserves; prior notice must be given and permits obtained for these. Private trips to the washes can, of course, be made; the cardinal sin here is to put to flight flocks of feeding or resting birds, so please do not walk along the banks or even show yourself over the tops. Washland bird watching requires a special technique of walking along under the river bank to the chosen spot and then peeping over the top into the washes. It is well worth the effort to be there and be able to enjoy the space, isolation and sheer remoteness of this unique area. The sound of a thousand Wigeon whistling under a frosty February moon or the sight of Bewick's Swans flighting under a fierce December sunset is never to be forgotten.

Wood Walton and Holme Fens

These two closely associated National Nature Reserves are managed by the Nature Conservancy Council. They are the only tracts of land in the western fens that are not now farmed and, as such, are of considerable ecological significance. The two reserves lie about 10 miles south-east of Peterborough and are a couple of miles apart.

Wood Walton Fen (500 acres) has a history of surface peat works with associated dyke cutting, coupled with mowing of litter and summer grazing. In the early 1900s, the fen was covered in reed and mixed wetland vegetation with very little shrub growth. Within twenty years the bushes had spread into the fen, suppressing the fen vegetation in several areas; a natural progression into sallow carr and scrub woodland would have followed without a management programme geared to the survival of typical fen habitats.

Current management aims are to improve the water regimes within the reserve, often by accepting flood water from the surrounding farmlands and so gradually to reduce the area of scrubland and rough carr. A wider range of habitats is being developed, including open stretches of water, and cattle have been introduced to graze some areas.

Where the sphagnum peat of the original bogland has not been removed, an acid heath flora still survives, including Bog Myrtle and Ling, plants not seen anywhere else in the area. The remaining peat is typical of the area—highly alkaline—holding a typical fen vegetation including the fen violet and the extremely rare Pale Woodrush (*Luzula pallescans*), which is found at both Wood Walton and Holme and at only one other site in Britain.

The reserve is probably best known for its insect life, particularly the colony of introduced Large Copper butterflies; it is the only place in Britain where this magnificent butterfly can be found.

Much long-term research is in progress on the reserve and casual visitors are not allowed; serious naturalists can however obtain a permit from the Nature Conservancy Council.

The slightly larger Holme Fen National Nature Reserve stands on the deep peat soils that once formed the edge of Whittlesey Mere. After the drainage of the Mere in 1851, Holme Fen came under the plough and by 1870 was dotted with coverts of mixed conifers and deciduous trees, probably planted originally as game cover. With the shrinkage of the peat, farming became more difficult and the trees began to take over, especially the birches, which by 1900 had almost covered the area. The reserve is still extensively wooded, mainly with birch in different stages of development, with alder in the damper spots and relic pines from the original game coverts. As at Wood Walton, the habitats are being extended, this time by peat extraction, thus lowering the land surface to form pools and reedbeds, similar to the conditions that must have been found when Whittlesey Mere was a vast freshwater lake.

The reserve holds many species of fenland and fen woodland plants, many of which can be seen from the public nature trail that is signposted through the fen. A recent invader is the Rose Bay Willow Herb, now colonising open glades as part of the birch woodland cycle. It has already been colonised in its turn by numbers of the Elephant Hawk Moth.

Probably the best known object in the fen is the famous Holme Post, a metal column that was driven flush into the peat in 1848 and which now stands many feet above the surface.

Other Sites and Habitats

The major nature reserves by no means exhaust the interest of the fens for the natural historian. The Wildfowl Trust maintains an excellent collection of ducks, geese and swans of over eighty species at Peakirk, near Peterborough, which offers an unrivalled opportunity to see all the native species at close quarters, thus aiding identification in the field. In conjunction with Peakirk, the Trust also operates a wildfowl ringing station at the nearby Borough Fen Decoy, a 2½-acre pool surrounded by 14 acres of quite dense woodland colonised by many species of small birds lacking such an environment in the rather bare fenland surroundings. The decoy is visited by quite large flocks of dabbling ducks and up to 2,000 of them are ringed each year, adding considerably to our knowledge of the movements of these species.

The washes of the Nene, stretching for 12 miles from Peterborough to Guyhirne and up to a mile wide, are similar in many respects to the Ouse Washes although flooding only occurs under very exceptional circumstances. Cultivation of the basin has been increasing in recent years, but flocks of Mallard, Teal, Wigeon and Pintail, as well as many waders, are still attracted to the scattered, low-lying marshes along the washes. Probably the most exciting time is when the large roost of Pink-footed Geese frequents the area in late winter, having moved in from the Holbeach salt marshes when feeding grounds there have become exhausted.

Chippenham Fen is a National Nature Reserve situated a few miles north of Newmarket. It lies in a small basin of low-lying land within the chalk and Breckland soils. Its 230 acres are criss-crossed by deep peat-cuttings, giving an even greater variety of habitat than can be seen at Wicken Fen. The reserve is well known for its relic fen vegetation and for the rare insect life to be found there.

Among the many other places within the Fens that the birdwatcher or botanist will find of interest are stretches of open water, often with shallow margins such as those at the settling pits of the beet sugar factories at Ely and Wissington and the gravel and clay workings along the fen margins, especially interesting pits being found at Fenstanton, Hemingford Grey, St Ives, Mepal and Waterbeach in the south, and at Sleaford, Tallington and Fletton in the north and west.

Hedgerows have never been particularly plentiful on the fens, particularly on the peatlands, but some very old examples do occur on parish boundaries. The Cambridgeshire and Isle of Ely Naturalists' Trust is conducting a survey into the age of hedgerows in its region. Where soil blowing takes place some farmers are planting up new hedges of fast growing willow; it will be interesting to plot the colonisation of these hedges by insects and birds and to compare the fauna with that of the traditional thorn hedge. Evergreen cover is scarce in the fens, roosting birds depending for shelter in winter on the scattered ivy clumps in old hedgerows, or on garden evergreens.

Ponds are rather few and far between, probably because of the easily available water supply in the dykes; as far as we know, no one has compared the ecology of the few examples with that of nearby channelled water, a study which might provide interesting data. Amphibia, especially frogs and toads, seem to be on the decline in the fens, as elsewhere, though it is difficult to know which are the factors that are causing their reduction. River-banks and dyke sides provide another important habitat for aquatic and semi-aquatic plants characteristic of the fenlands. It would be useful to plot the distribution of such plants at the borders of peat and silt fen, and also where the freshwater drains gradually merge with the tidal salt marshes in the north.

Throughout the Fens, fishing is a major sport, and a good sample of the population is obtained by this activity; this is coarse fishing country, the slow moving muddy waters being eminently suitable for bream, roach, pike and tench. Eels are plentiful, often to the dismay of the match fisher, as only the specimen hunting *aficionado* is usually interested in this species. A new introduction to Fenland is the Zander, or pike-perch, a hybrid sporting fish common in the Netherlands and now to be found in many of the more eastern fen waters, weighing up to several pounds. Whether it will compete with the native pike or affect the stocks of smaller species has yet to be seen.

Insects, Mammals and Birds

Opportunity exists for much detailed work on the insect population and flora of the fen droves; these green trackways, often four cart-widths wide, cover miles of fen, many in remote and seldom visited areas. It is possible that quite exciting discoveries could be made by any determined naturalist. For example, in 1972 a small colony of the ragwort (*Senecio paludosus*) was found in the Cambridgeshire fens. The plant was last recorded at Wicken in 1857 and was thought to be extinct in Britain, but fresh ditch digging apparently stimulated the germination of seed that had lain dormant in the peat for many years. The mammal population, too, both of the droveways and the open fen, has scarcely been charted. Foxes, weasels and stoats are common in many areas; foxes are particularly to be seen where there are isolated coverts and woodlands, though they are not averse to copying their town cousins' habits and raiding dustbins and hen runs at night. Rabbits are becoming more plentiful and even seem to have escaped the ravages of myxomatosis altogether in the more remote areas.

Of the recently introduced species, the coypu has declined under a drastic trapping programme but is still seen from time to time. Mink are present on the fen, occasionally breeding on the banks of the larger rivers and hunting over an area of many square miles.

Bats are common all over the region but very little seems to have been published concerning the status of the various species. Without doubt, many of the church towers and hollow trees around the fens house colonies of these interesting animals; it is difficult to assess the strength of the populations, but it is likely that the decline in the number of bats experienced over the country as a whole may not be quite so severe in the Fens.

The status of snakes in the Fens is also very difficult to assess, and would repay deeper study. Grass snakes are regularly seen, but the adder and the smooth snake are apparently fewer in number, as might be expected. Towards the Breckland, in the east, the adder might find conditions more suitable.

Several changes are taking place in the bird-life of the

cultivated fenlands, the most striking being the colonisation of many areas, particularly around grain stores and villages, by the Collared Dove, which from a first British breeding record in 1956, has now become quite a pest. The closely related Turtle Dove also seems to be increasing in numbers, albeit rather more slowly.

The Cuckoo, Yellow Hammer, Reed Bunting and Bullfinch all seem to be on an upward trend at the moment; the Reed Bunting increase is perhaps linked with a very subtle change of habitat, for this species seems to be spreading out of the reed beds and into the cornfields.

Birds of prey have suffered, as elsewhere, from pesticide build-up, but happily the Kestrel population now seems to be recovering and Sparrow Hawks can occasionally be seen in the more wooded parts of the Fens. Barn Owls are now one of the typical fenland species and are present in some areas in quite considerable numbers.

Of the warblers, the fens are more suited to the Reed and Sedge Warblers than many of the other species; both are common and doing well. In the denser thickets of fenland the Nightingale is quite common and, in one area at least, the Golden Oriole is known to have been present during the breeding season.

A feature of the winter landscape is the large number of thrush species, Fieldfare and Redwing in particular, which together with Lapwings and Gulls feed on the arable and grassland fields.

An aspect of bird life that might reveal some surprising facts would be a study of migratory patterns over the Fens, following the lines of a sea watch from the coast. Using this technique from suitable vantage points, migrating flocks and single passage birds could be plotted, from the June influx of Dutch Lapwings to the autumn passage of waders, Kestrels and larger raptors.

With migration in mind, it is perhaps relevant to mention here the varied bird life to be found on the

Fenland coast. This wild no-man's-land of mud, marsh and sky, stretching around the Wash from King's Lynn to Skegness, is the haunt of large flocks of geese, ducks and wading birds during winter and at passage times. In summer the salt marsh vegetation provides ample cover for the commoner breeding species of duck and waders. Beyond the coastline, the sand and mud banks of the Wash provide a breeding ground for the Common Seal, now the subject of a controversial annual cull. The popular local delicacy, samphire (*Salicornia europaea*), is found on the salt marshes and is still harvested and sold on market stalls as far inland as Ely and Cambridge.

This chapter seems to have thrown up more questions than answers, which will perhaps serve to stimulate the naturalist to visit the Fens and to raise interest in the area, parts of which are virtually unsurveyed by scientific workers.

Bibliography

A General

The Fenland occupies parts of several counties (some of which are now amalgamated) so books on Cambridgeshire and the Isle of Ely, Huntingdonshire, Lincolnshire, Norfolk, Northamptonshire (Soke of Peterborough) and Suffolk may all be relevant. The following series are especially valuable.

The Buildings of England
Pevsner, N. *Bedfordshire and the County of Huntingdon and Peterborough* (Harmondsworth 1968)
——. *Cambridgeshire* (2nd edn Harmondsworth 1970)
——. and Harris, J. *Lincolnshire* (Harmondsworth 1964)
——. *North-west and South Norfolk* (Harmondsworth 1962)
——. revised by Ratcliffe, E. *Suffolk* (2nd edn Harmondsworth 1975)

Inventories of the Royal Commission on Historical Monuments
City of Cambridge, 2 vols and maps (1959)
North-East Cambridgeshire (1972)
Huntingdonshire (1926)
Peterborough New Town—a survey of the antiquities in the areas of development (1969)

The Victoria County History of England
Cambridgeshire and the Isle of Ely, 5 vols and index to vols 1–4 (1938–73)

Huntingdonshire, 3 vols and index (1926–38)
Lincolnshire, Vol 2 only (1906)
Norfolk, 2 vols (1901–6)
Northamptonshire, 4 vols (1902–37)

The Agrarian History of England and Wales
Finberg, H P R (ed) Vol I.2 *AD 43–1042* (1972)
Thirsk, Joan (ed) Vol IV *1500–1640* (1967)

English Place-name Society
Reaney, P H *The Place-names of Cambridgeshire and the Isle of Ely* (1943)
Gover, J E B, Mawer, A and Stenton, F M *The Place-names of Northamptonshire* (1933)

The following books, though not specifically on any part of the Fenland, are important to an understanding of particular aspects of it:
Barley, M W *The English Farmhouse and Cottage* (1961)
Clifton-Taylor, A *English Parish Churches as Works of Art* (1974)
——. *The Pattern of English Building* (1972)
Crossley, F H *The English Abbey* (2nd edn 1939)
Ernle, R E P *English Farming Past and Present* (6th edn 1961)
Frere, S S *Britannia* (1967)
Margary, I D *Roman Roads in Britain* (3rd edn 1963)
Myres, J N L *Anglo-Saxon Pottery and the Settlement of England* (1969)
Willan, T S *River Navigation in England 1600–1750* (1936)

B Specific (*Booklets are marked with an asterisk*)

Allen, C J *The Great Eastern Railway* (5th edn Shepperton 1968)
Astbury, A K *The Black Fens* (Cambridge 1958, reprinted Wakefield 1970)

BIBLIOGRAPHY

Barley, M W *Lincolnshire and the Fens* (1952, reprinted Wakefield 1972)

Barrett, W H (ed Porter, Enid) *Tales from the Fens* (1963)

——. *More Tales from the Fens* (1964)

——. *A Fenman's Story* (1965)

Bloom, A H V *The Farm in the Fen* (1944)

——. *The Fens* (1953)

——. *The Skaters of the Fens* (Cambridge 1958)

Booth, P and Taylor, N *Cambridge New Architecture* (1970)

——. *A Guide to Cambridge New Architecture* (1972)

Braithwaite, D *Savage of King's Lynn, inventor of machines and merry-go-rounds* (Bar Hill 1975)

Cambridgeshire and Isle of Ely Naturalists' Trust Handbook of Nature Reserves (Cambridge 1970)

Clark, R H *Short History of the Midland and Great Northern Joint Railway* (Norwich 1967)

Darby, H C (ed) *The Cambridge Region* (1938)

——. *The Medieval Fenland* (1940, reprinted Newton Abbot 1974)

——. *The Domesday Geography of Eastern England* (1952)

——. *The Draining of the Fens* (2nd edn 1956)

Day, J W *A History of the Fens, their swamps, meres, men, sports, ducks, decoys, drainage, riots, floods, legends, fish and fowl* (1954, reprinted Wakefield 1970)

Dring, W E Fenland Story: from prehistoric times to the present day (2nd edn Cambridge 1967)

——. The Fen and the Furrow: books on South Cambridgeshire and the Fenland in the County Library (Cambridge 1974)

Ennion, E A R *Adventurers Fen* (2nd edn 1949)

Fenland Notes and Queries: a quarterly antiquarian journal for the Fenland in the counties of Huntingdon, Cambridge, Lincoln, Northampton, Norfolk and Suffolk (Peterborough 1889–1909)

Fox, C The Archaeology of the Cambridge Region (1923)

Gadsden, E J S et al The Wisbech and Upwell Tramway (Teddington 1967)

Gordon, D I Regional History of the Railways of Great Britain Vol 5 Eastern Counties (Newton Abbot 1968)

*Great Ouse River Authority Illustrated Handbook (Gloucester nd)

Grigg, D. The Agricultural Revolution in South Lincolnshire (1966)

Hallam, H E Settlement and Society: a study of the early agrarian history of South Lincolnshire (1965)

*Hey, R W and Perrin, R M S The Geology and Soils of Cambridgeshire (Cambridge 1960)

Hills, R L Machines, Mills and Uncountable Costly Necessities: a short history of the drainage of the Fens (Norwich 1967)

*Hinde, K S G Steam in the Fens (Cambridge 1974)

Holmes, R and Rouse, M Ely:Cathedral City and Market Town: a pictorial record 1817-1934 (Ely 1972)

Lucas, C The Fenman's World: memories of a Fenland physician (Norwich 1930)

Marlowe, C The Fen Country (1925)

——. Legends of the Fenland People (1926)

——. People and Places in Marshland (1927)

Marshall, S Fenland Chronicle; recollections of William Henry and Kate Mary Edwards (1967)

*Mason, H J Introduction to the Black Fens (Ely 1973)

Miller, E. The Abbey and Bishopric of Ely (1951)

*National Trust Wicken Fen Local Committee Wicken Fen [a series of ten guides on particular aspects of the Fen]

Nock, O S The Great Northern Railway (1958)

Parker, Vanessa The Making of King's Lynn (Chichester 1971)

Phillips, C W (ed) The Fenland in Roman Times (1970)

Porter, Enid M Cambridgeshire Customs and Folklore (1969)

Purcell, D Cambridge Stone (1967)

BIBLIOGRAPHY

Randell, A *Sixty Years a Fenman* (1966)

——. (ed Porter, Enid) *Fenland Railwayman* (1968)

——. (ed Porter, Enid) *Fenland Memories* (1969)

——. (ed Porter, Enid) *Fenland Molecatcher* (1970)

Ravensdale, J R *Liable to Floods: village landscape on the edge of the Fens AD 450–1850* (1974) [Landbeach, Waterbeach and Cottenham]

Rogers, A *History of Lincolnshire* (Henley-on-Thames 1970)

Roper, Lanning *The Gardens of Anglesey Abbey* (1964)

Skertchly, S B J & Miller, S H *The Fenland; past and present* (Wisbech 1878)

Spufford, M *Contrasting Communities: English villagers in the sixteenth and seventeenth centuries* (1974) [Willingham, Orwell and Chippenham]

Steers, J A (ed) *The Cambridge Region 1965* (Cambridge 1965)

Storey, E. *Portrait of the Fen Country* (1971)

Summers, D *Great Ouse: the history of a river navigation* (Newton Abbot 1973)

Taylor, C. *The Cambridgeshire Landscape* (1973)

Thirsk, Joan *Fenland Farming in the Sixteenth Century* (Leicester 1953)

——. *English Peasant Farming: the agrarian history of Lincolnshire from Tudor to recent times* (1957)

Tibbs, R. *Fenland River: the story of the Great Ouse and its tributaries* (Lavenham 1969)

Tombleson, P. *The Fens* (Peterborough 1962) [Fishing]

Walford, C *Fairs, Past and Present* (1883) [History of Stourbridge Fair]

Wedgwood, Iris V. *Fenland Rivers: impressions of the Fen counties* (1936)

Wheeler, W H *A History of the Fens of South Lincolnshire* (2nd edn Boston 1896)

Whitwell, J B *Roman Lincolnshire* (Lincoln 1970)

*Wicken Fen Group *Birds at Wicken, Annual Report* (1970–)

Willis, R & Clark, J W *The Architectural History of the*

BIBLIOGRAPHY

University of Cambridge and of the Colleges of Cambridge and Eton, 4 vols (1886)

Willock, C. D. *Kenzie; the wild goose man* (1962)

*Wilson, J K *Fenland Barge Traffic* (Kettering 1972)

*Wright, C H and Ward, J F *A Survey of the Soils and Fruit of the Wisbech Area* (Harpenden 1929)

Wrottesley, A J *Midland and Great Northern Joint Railway* (Newton Abbot 1970)

Index

237

INDEX

INDEX